– ED. U.S.A.
BROS?

First published in the U.S.A. in 1977 by Crown Publishers, Inc.
© S. F. King 1977
Library of Congress Catalog Card Number 77-5598
ISBN 0-517-529432

Made and Printed in Italy

Filmset by Thomson Litho Ltd, East Kilbride, Scotland
in 11/12 point Bembo (with modern figures).

THE INTERNATIONAL
DOLLS HOUSE
BOOK

Contents

Photographs by Edmund Dwyer

THE INTERNATIONAL
DOLLS HOUSE
BOOK

S.F.KING

Crown Publishers Inc.
New York

Before you begin

This book has been designed for the handy man and woman who can measure fairly accurately, use a hand saw and have a modicum of commonsense.

Dolls houses are not difficult to make and it is even possible to hide mistakes and errors (provided they are not too bad) by the judicious use of cellulose wood filler or plastic wood. Select the dolls house you want to make and collect your tools and materials. Before you begin read the following instructions carefully and bear them in mind while constructing your house, its furniture and, perhaps, its garden.

The designs described here are for the houses shown in the photographs. They are basic designs and can easily be altered to suit your own needs. If you do adapt a design, think through the consequences of the alteration; for example, how it will affect the sizes and shapes of the other pieces of wood.

Measurements
The drawings for the houses are to scale. The dimensions are given in both metric and imperial units. Use either of these, but **do not mix the units** —stick to either metric or imperial units throughout. All necessary measurements are given, but, as the drawings are to scale, you can use measurements taken from the drawings to find any other dimensions. For example, if a drawing is 1:5 scale and a part measures 2.5cm (1″) on the drawing, it will be 2.5 (1″) × 5 = 12.5cm (5″) on the house.

Tools
Do not clutter yourself with too many tools. Those you do need should be of good quality and sharp where they need to be. 'A good workman never blames his tools', but even the best workman cannot do a good job with poor quality, blunt tools. The following is a list of the essential tools.
    fine-toothed tenon saw
    fretsaw, with a supply of medium blades
    hand drill with bits
    sandpaper
    fretsaw table (to clamp to working surface)
    lightweight hammer
    try square
    steel rule

    6mm ($\frac{1}{4}$″) and 1.2cm ($\frac{1}{2}$″) chisels
    padsaw or keyhole saw
    craft knife with a supply of spare blades
    tracing paper and thin card
    woodworking adhesive
    small screwdriver
    paintbrushes

These are useful additional tools.
    clamps to hold pieces together while glue sets
    small block plane
    mitre box for cutting ends of wood square
    (particularly when making the Japanese house)
    vice

Materials
The main material used in these dolls houses is plywood, 3mm ($\frac{1}{8}$″) and 6mm ($\frac{1}{4}$″) thick. Use birch-faced ply. It may be slightly more expensive than other plywoods, but it is easier to cut, does not splinter or split easily, and has a good surface for painting.

In the materials lists the amount of plywood is given in standard sheets of 240 × 120cm (8′ × 4′). It is cheaper to buy standard sheets than pieces cut to size, although you can sometimes buy offcuts quite cheaply.

Before marking out the wood, check that its thickness is **exactly** that stated in the text and on the drawings. You will sometimes find that wood is not exactly cut to size. You must make allowances for these differences when you mark out the pieces for making the houses.

Marking out patterns
When marking out the wood, plan how the pieces can best be laid out to avoid wasting wood. Use a try square to make sure your marking out is square and that lines that should be parallel really are. After marking out and before cutting out, think about how the various pieces are going to fit together.

Cutting out
Use a fine-toothed tenon saw for cutting the main pieces. Rest the sheet on boxes or on a table while cutting. It is helpful if somebody can hold the piece of wood that is being cut off, particularly when the cut is nearly complete. If using a power saw use the finest blade available, or you will get a very rough edge. When cutting the 3mm ($\frac{1}{8}$″) ply, score along the lines with a sharp craft knife, using a steel rule

as a cutting guide. It is quite easy to cut the wood right through with a craft knife, and you will get a very smooth edge.

Use a medium blade fretsaw to cut the window openings. First drill a small hole near one corner of the window opening, unclamp the fretsaw blade at the handle end, feed it through the hole, and reclamp the blade. Remember not to force the blade and to keep it upright. You could use a padsaw or keyhole saw, though these may give a rougher edge.

After cutting out, smooth down all edges with a medium grade sandpaper. When smoothing flat surfaces, sandpaper with the grain. To give a really smooth surface for painting or staining, give a final rub down with very fine sandpaper.

Assembling the parts

Use fine panel pins 1.2cm ($\frac{1}{2}''$) long to fix the various parts together. Draw guidelines on both surfaces of the wood. Use a lightweight hammer to hammer in the pin and make sure the pin is absolutely vertical. Use a good quality woodworking adhesive and follow the manufacturer's instructions to the letter. Modern adhesives used properly produce very powerful bonds. The pins only hold the wood together, and cannot by themselves give much strength to the join. Check before the glue sets that the pieces are square. Do be patient; wait until the glue has really set before proceeding further. Do not be in too much of a hurry to fix all the pieces together. For example, hinge the doors and windows in place and trim, if necessary, to give a good fit. Remove them and decorate them. Refix them in position after all the walls and rooms have been decorated.

In some of the designs the window frames (and shutters in the Swiss Chalet) are made from balsa wood. Use hard balsa: you can feel whether the balsa is hard or not. Carefully trace the design on a sheet of paper. Cover this with greaseproof paper. Build the frame directly over the pattern on the grease-proof paper. Use balsa cement to hold the parts together and, while the cement is setting, use pins to keep the pieces correctly aligned. (Greaseproof paper is used because the cement will not stick to it, so the frame can be lifted off when the cement has set.)

Painting

Generally, gloss enamel paints are not suitable for dolls houses. Use vinyl silk emulsion, which gives a surface that looks good and can easily be cleaned with a damp cloth. In order to avoid buying many tins of different coloured paints, use white paint and tint small quantities with powder colour or poster colour. Make sure you mix up sufficient paint to give two or three coats to the surface, and keep the paint in a jar with a screw-top so that it will not dry up between coats.

Where the windows or lintels are a different colour from the outer walls, fix them in place only after they have been decorated (and glazed in the case of the windows) and all other decorating, interior and exterior, has been completed.

Papering the walls

Use wallpaper specially made for dolls houses or gift wrapping paper. Ordinary wallpaper is unsuitable. Choose carefully so that any pattern on the paper does not look out-of-place. Narrow striped and plain papers are good.

Cut out a piece of paper slightly larger than the wall to be covered. Cover the back of paper liberally with wallpaper paste. Put the pasted paper on the wall, covering window and door openings, and line up at the ceiling edge. Carefully smooth out the paper from the centre to get rid of creases and air bubbles. When the paste is absolutely dry cut out window and door openings with a sharp knife.

Furniture

Most furniture patterns are shown full size so that you can trace them. After cutting out the pieces, smooth down all rough edges. Check to see that the pieces fit together properly. Using a wood adhesive sparingly, glue the parts together, and check for squareness. Remove excess glue with a damp cloth before it sets hard.

All the dolls houses are built to the standard scale of 1:12. This means that the furniture for the various houses is interchangeable.

The gardens

The gardens designed for the Hacienda and the Japanese House are only suggestions that can easily be varied. The gardens are not essential to the houses, but certainly provide extra play value.

THE SWISS CHALET

This design is based (at least externally) on the Swiss chalets often seen in the Engadine. These chalets are charming, with their window boxes gay with geraniums and other flowers, and yet seem to reflect the solidity, firmness and common sense of the Swiss people. The walls are built from local stone, and the roof, floors, ceilings, doors and window frames are made from pinewood. The pitch of the roof is low, about 30°, to stop the snow sliding off; the layer of snow acts as a good heat insulator during the winter.

The dolls house is planned to the traditional scale of 1:12. This scale produces quite a reasonable-sized house with four good rooms, a basement for storage and a large attic, which could be used as a nursery or playroom.

The house, including the roof, is made from plywood; 6mm ($\frac{1}{4}$″) is a suitable thickness. One standard sheet approximately 240 × 120cm (8′ × 4′) will be sufficient. In fact, you should have about one third of the sheet left. (With careful marking out you can also make the Gypsy Caravan, described later in the book, from the same sheet of plywood.) The measurements given in the text and on the drawings are all based on the use of 6mm ($\frac{1}{4}$″) plywood. You can use thicker ply, but, if you do, you will have to adapt the design; for example, you would have to make the floors narrower because they must fit between the two side walls.

Balsa wood is used to make the window frames and window boxes ; the flowers are made of tissue paper.

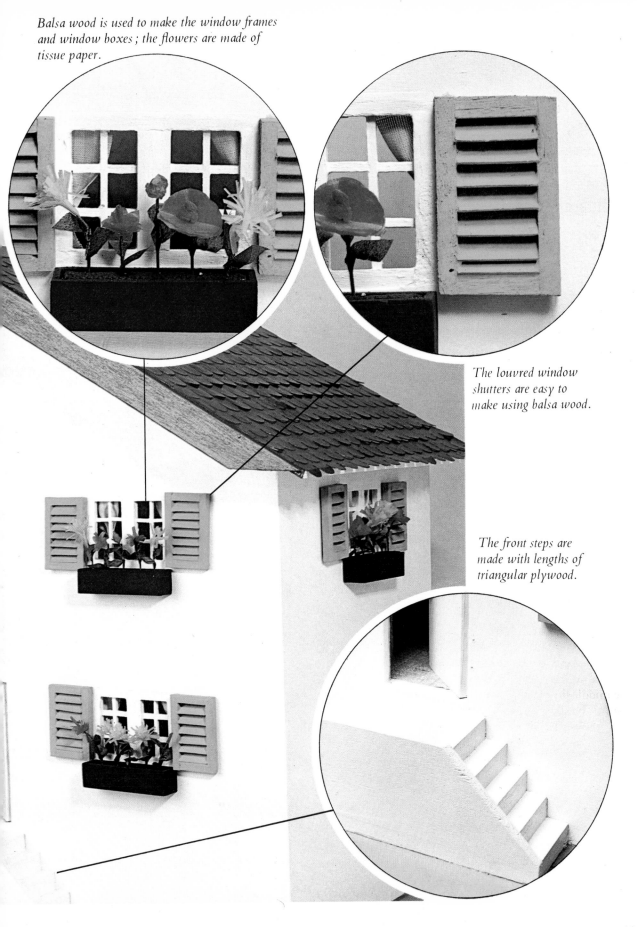

The louvred window shutters are easy to make using balsa wood.

The front steps are made with lengths of triangular plywood.

Building
the chalet

Materials

1 sheet 6mm ($\frac{1}{4}''$) plywood 240×120cm ($8' \times 4'$)
6mm ($\frac{1}{4}''$) square balsa wood
3mm ($\frac{1}{8}''$) square balsa wood
3mm ($\frac{1}{8}''$) sheet balsa wood
2cm ($\frac{3}{4}''$) triangular section wood
2 sheets white card 64×52cm ($26'' \times 21''$)
woodworking glue and fabric adhesive
1.2cm or 1.8cm ($\frac{1}{2}''$ or $\frac{3}{4}''$) panel pins
2 2.5cm ($1''$) hinges
8 6mm ($\frac{1}{4}''$) brass screws
fabric, foam rubber, paint

The basic structure

Mark out front as shown and cut out. Drill holes in window and door openings, and then use a fret saw to cut round lines you have drawn.

Mark position of walls and tops of floors, as shown by the broken lines, on both sides of front.

Cut front door and fix in position with a pair of 2.5cm ($1''$) hinges and 6mm ($\frac{1}{4}''$) brass screws. Check that door opens and closes easily. Oil hinges slightly.

Mark out and cut two side walls. Smooth down any rough edges on sides and front with sandpaper. Glue and pin front to sides. Use a good woodworking adhesive and follow the manufacturer's instructions. Punch down pin heads with small nail punch so they can be covered with filler later. Check that side walls are square with front before glue sets.

Make three floors. They are all the same size, but:
the lower floor has two slots, cut as shown (these will be at the rear of the house when slotted into the internal walls);
the middle floor has the same two slots and an opening for the staircase cut next to one slot;
the top floor has no slots or openings.
Smooth down any rough edges with sandpaper.

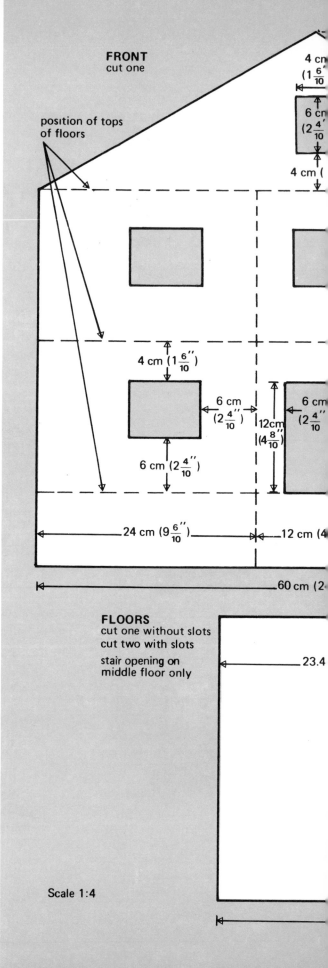

FRONT
cut one

position of tops
of floors

4 cm
($1\frac{6}{10}''$)

6 cm
($2\frac{4}{10}''$)

4 cm (

4 cm ($1\frac{6}{10}''$)

6 cm
($2\frac{4}{10}''$)

6 cm
($2\frac{4}{10}''$)

12cm
($4\frac{8}{10}''$)

6 cm ($2\frac{4}{10}''$)

24 cm ($9\frac{6}{10}''$)

12 cm (4

60 cm (2

FLOORS
cut one without slots
cut two with slots

stair opening on
middle floor only

23.4

Scale 1:4

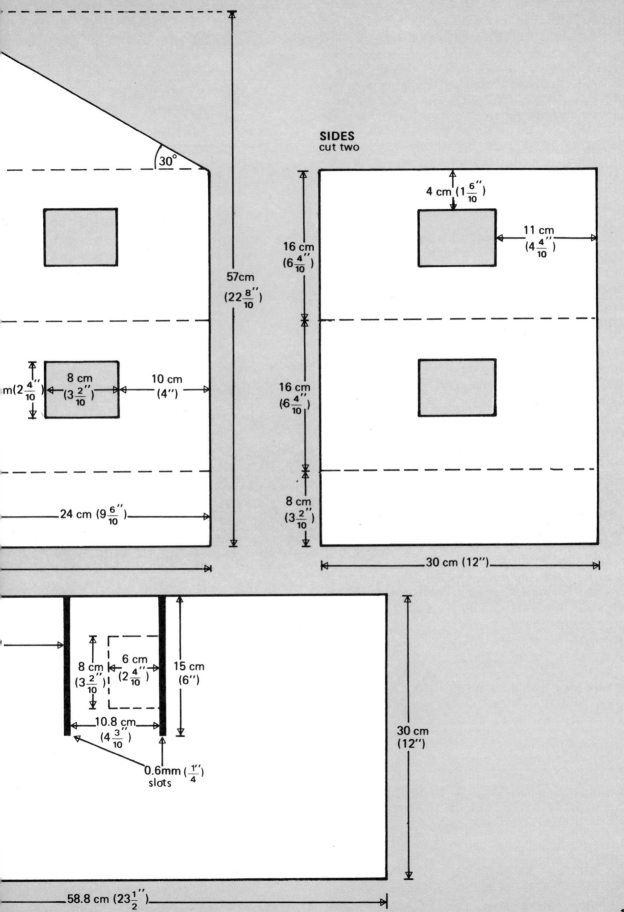

30°

57cm
$(22\frac{8}{10}'')$

m$(2\frac{4}{10}'')$

8 cm
$(3\frac{2}{10}'')$

10 cm
$(4'')$

24 cm $(9\frac{6}{10}'')$

SIDES
cut two

4 cm $(1\frac{6}{10}'')$

11 cm
$(4\frac{4}{10}'')$

16 cm
$(6\frac{4}{10}'')$

16 cm
$(6\frac{4}{10}'')$

8 cm
$(3\frac{2}{10}'')$

30 cm $(12'')$

8 cm
$(3\frac{2}{10}'')$

6 cm
$(2\frac{4}{10}'')$

15 cm
$(6'')$

10.8 cm
$(4\frac{3}{10}'')$

0.6mm $(\frac{1}{4}'')$
slots

30 cm
$(12'')$

58.8 cm $(23\frac{1}{2}'')$

Internal walls

Mark out and cut out two dividing walls as shown. Cut out door openings. Smooth down any rough edges with medium sandpaper. Check that lower and middle floors slot into two dividing walls as shown. Glue them together, checking that they are all square to one another. Let glue dry.

Put this structure between the two side walls so that the walls and tops of the floors align with the lines you have drawn to show their positions. When everything is aligned, glue and pin the internal walls to the front and sides. Glue and pin the top floor in position.

Roof and base

Cut a piece of 6mm ($\frac{1}{4}''$) plywood 70×50cm ($28'' \times 20''$) for the base. Cut two pieces 41×35cm ($16\frac{4}{10}'' \times 14''$) for the two halves of the roof. Cut out the rear roof support as shown, and fix it to the rear edge of the top floor. Pin and glue the two roof halves in position; the rear edges of the 41cm ($16\frac{4}{10}''$) width are flush with the edge of the rear roof support, and the front edges overlap the front of the house.

You can chamfer the edges where the two roof halves meet so that they fit flush with one another, but this is not absolutely necessary, as the join will be covered with card later.

Now fix the house to the base. You will probably need some help doing this. Position the rear of the house flush with the edge of the base. The base extends out the front and sides for the path and garden. Viewing the house from the rear, it should look like the diagram opposite. Punch down all nail heads and rub down surfaces and edges with sandpaper before painting the house.

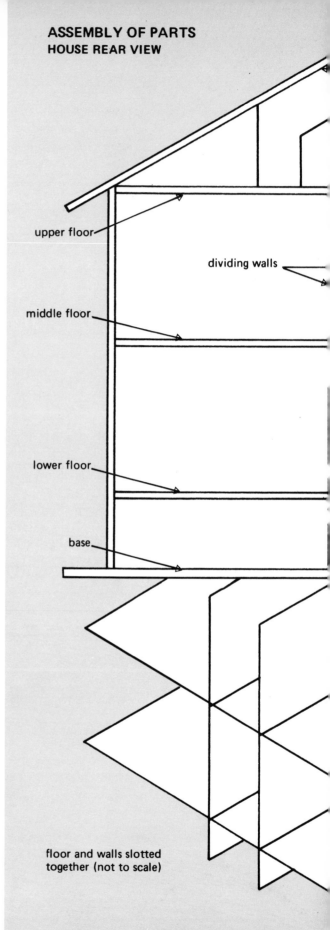

ASSEMBLY OF PARTS
HOUSE REAR VIEW

upper floor

dividing walls

middle floor

lower floor

base

floor and walls slotted together (not to scale)

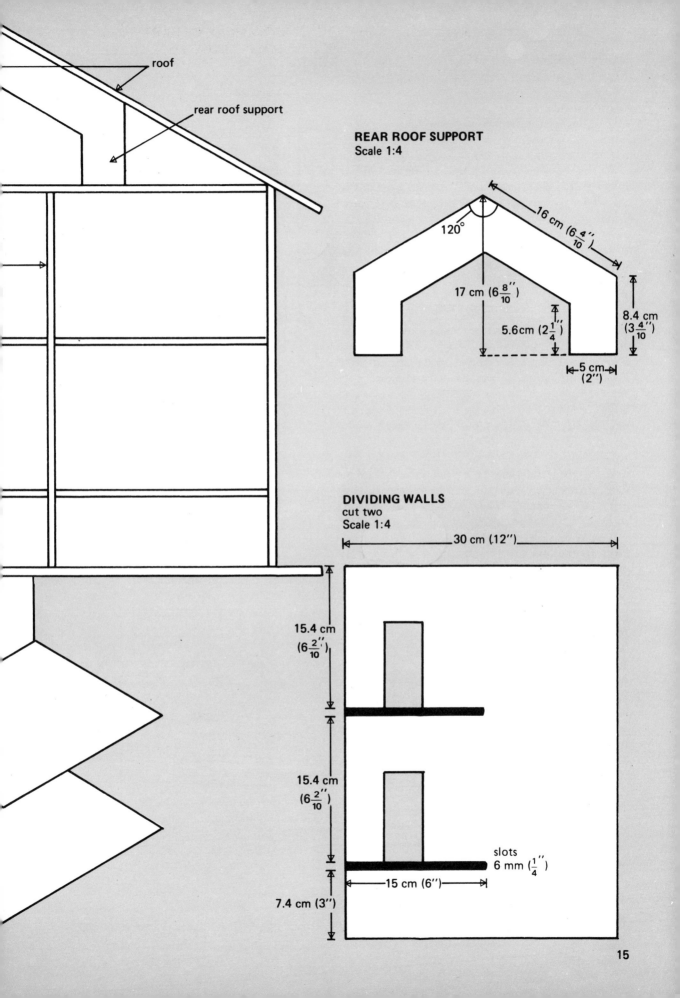

roof

rear roof support

REAR ROOF SUPPORT
Scale 1:4

120°

16 cm ($6\frac{4}{10}''$)

17 cm ($6\frac{8}{10}''$)

8.4 cm ($3\frac{4}{10}''$)

5.6 cm ($2\frac{1}{4}''$)

5 cm (2'')

DIVIDING WALLS
cut two
Scale 1:4

30 cm (12'')

15.4 cm ($6\frac{2}{10}''$)

15.4 cm ($6\frac{2}{10}''$)

slots
6 mm ($\frac{1}{4}''$)

15 cm (6'')

7.4 cm (3'')

15

All the diagrams opposite are actual size and can be traced to provide accurate working guides.

Window frames

Cut 6mm ($\frac{1}{4}''$) square balsa to size to make outer frame. Glue pieces together with balsa cement, holding in place with pins until cement has set. Cut inner frames from 3mm ($\frac{1}{8}''$) square balsa. Glue in place. When glue has set hard, smooth wood with very fine sandpaper. Make 8 double and 2 single windows.

Check that the frames fit the window openings. If they are too big, remove excess with sandpaper. If they are too small, you can glue them in place and fill the gaps before painting the house exterior.

Give all window frames two or three coats of white emulsion paint; vinyl matt and vinyl silk paints give a very good finish. You may need to smooth the frames with sandpaper between coats of paint.

Glue the frames in place, flush with the walls. Fill any gaps with a suitable filler.

Shutters

Cut out frames for 16 shutters from 6mm ($\frac{1}{4}''$) square balsa. Cut 7 louvres for each shutter from balsa sheet 1mm ($\frac{1}{16}''$) or thinner. Glue the frames together and let dry. Glue louvres in frames at an angle, using the side view diagram as a guide.

Window boxes

Cut the pieces shown from 3mm ($\frac{1}{8}''$) sheet balsa. Glue the ends to the bottom, then glue on sides. Make eight boxes. Insert blocks of polystyrene foam for soil.

Roof scallops

Mark a sheet of thin card in 2cm ($\frac{8}{10}''$) strips 41cm (16$\frac{4}{10}''$) long. Cut out one scalloped strip as shown opposite; use it as a template to cut out 37 more strips. Starting at the eaves, glue 19 strips to each half of roof so that they overlap and scallops alternate. Fold card 8 × 41cm (3″ × 16$\frac{4}{10}''$) in half lengthways and glue over roof join.

Barge boards

Cut two pieces 4 × 35cm (1$\frac{6}{10}''$ × 14″) from 6mm ($\frac{1}{4}''$) ply. Glue under front eaves of roof. Make a finial from 2cm ($\frac{8}{10}''$) radius circle of wood and glue over the join (see photo, pages 10-11).

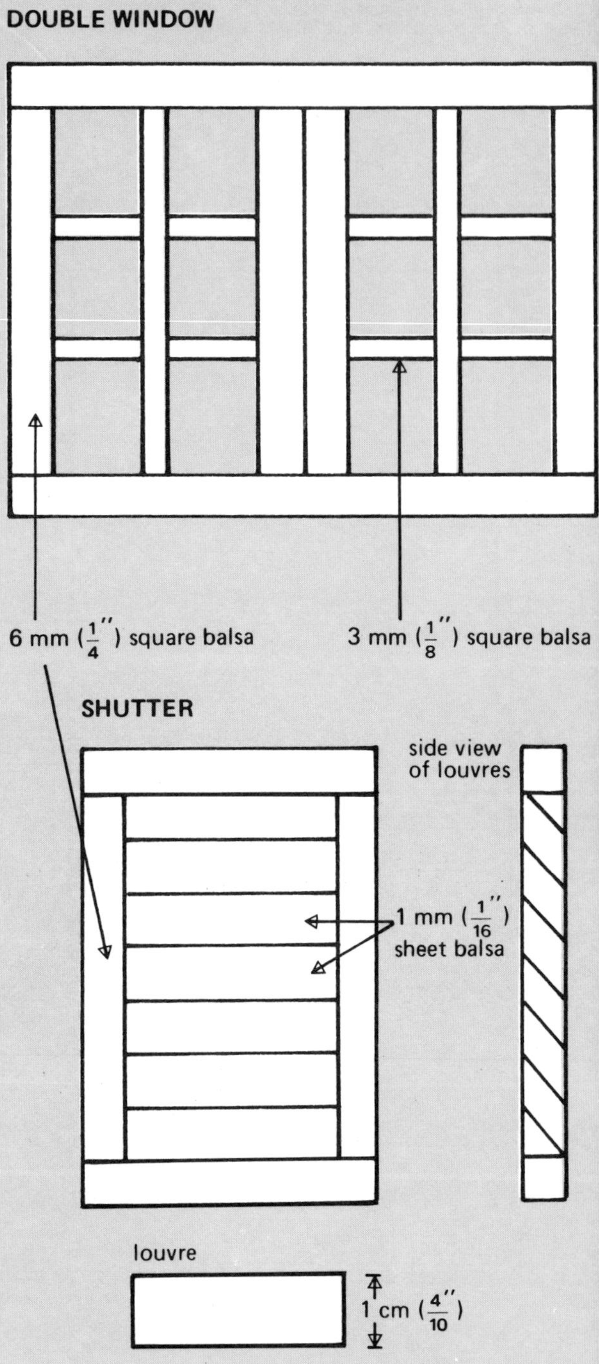

DOUBLE WINDOW

6 mm ($\frac{1}{4}''$) square balsa

3 mm ($\frac{1}{8}''$) square balsa

SHUTTER

side view of louvres

1 mm ($\frac{1}{16}''$) sheet balsa

louvre

1 cm ($\frac{4}{10}''$)

WINDOW BOX CONSTRUCTION

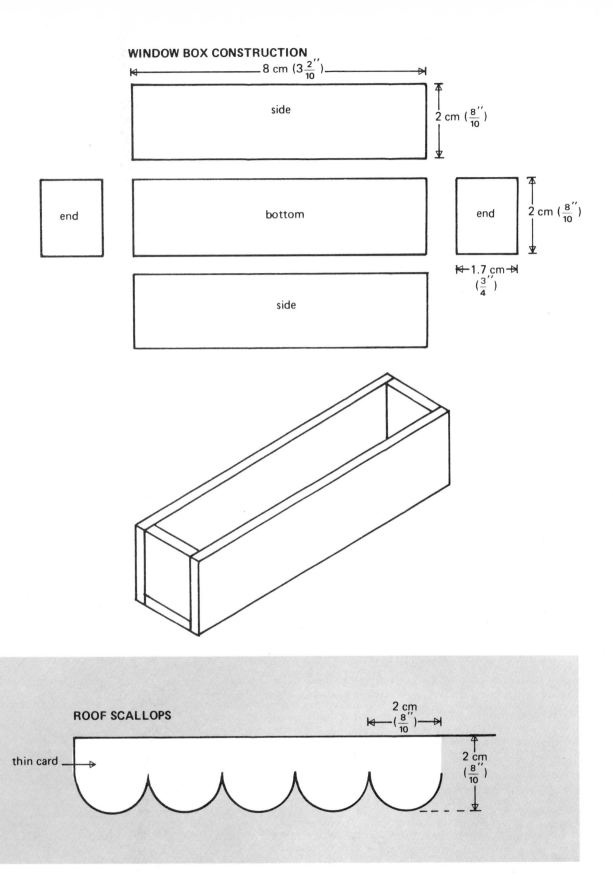

8 cm $(3\frac{2}{10}'')$

side

2 cm $(\frac{8''}{10})$

end

bottom

end

2 cm $(\frac{8''}{10})$

1.7 cm $(\frac{3}{4}'')$

side

ROOF SCALLOPS

thin card

2 cm $(\frac{8''}{10})$

2 cm $(\frac{8''}{10})$

Front steps

Using 6mm ($\frac{1}{4}$″) ply cut two pieces 6 × 8cm ($2\frac{4}{10}$″ × $3\frac{2}{10}$″). Stick five 6cm ($2\frac{4}{10}$″) lengths of triangular wood to each piece. Trim ends of ply as shown in diagram. Cut a piece of ply to shape shown by broken line. Pin and glue strips of steps to this piece as shown. Add landing piece at top, measuring directly from your model.

Stairs

These are made in a similar way to front steps. Cut strip of ply 6 × 18cm ($2\frac{4}{10}$″ × $7\frac{2}{10}$″). Glue on ten 6cm ($2\frac{4}{10}$″) lengths of triangular wood. Cut ply to shape shown by broken line. Pin and glue stairs to it. Fix landing in place, measuring piece from your model. Paint with two coats white emulsion. Fix in place *after* decorating house inside.

Decorating and finishing

Give the outside walls 2–3 coats white emulsion. Glue the front stairs in place and paint white. Paint the roof dark brown and cover with 1–2 coats polyurethane varnish. This looks nice and allows the roof to be cleaned with a damp cloth. Paint shutters leaf green and window boxes brown, using white emulsion coloured with poster paint. Glue shutters and window boxes in place. Paint the base green with a brown path along the front of the house.

Make flowers from coloured tissue paper. Cut 5cm (2″) lengths of green florist's wire. Cut tissue paper 1 × 6cm ($\frac{4}{10}$″ × $2\frac{4}{10}$″), and cut fringe in long edge. Dab glue on long uncut edge and roll strip around top of wire. When dry, ease out 'petals'. Add green tissue paper leaves 1.5 × 1cm ($\frac{1}{2}$″ × $\frac{4}{10}$″). Make buds by crumpling tissue paper into balls and gluing to stem. Push stems into window box soil.

Inside the house the ceilings can be painted white or left plain. Wallpaper specially made for dolls houses can be bought at model or do-it-yourself shops. You can also use gift wrapping paper with very small patterns, but do not use full-size patterned wallpaper, which is out of scale.

Cut wallpaper for each wall. Cover the back liberally with wallpaper paste and place on wall, smoothing outwards from the centre to get rid of bubbles and creases. Trim off excess when paste is dry.

Paint floors or cover with self-adhesive vinyl, selecting suitable patterns.

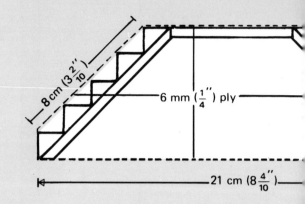

FRONT STEPS
Scale 1:2

8cm ($3\frac{2}{10}$″)

6 mm ($\frac{1}{4}$″) ply

21 cm ($8\frac{4}{10}$″)

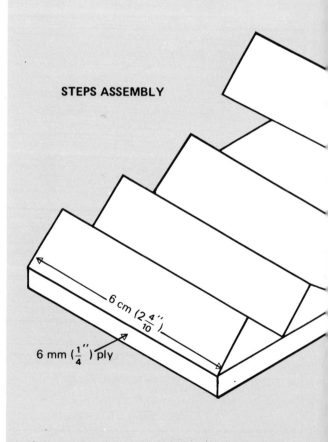

STEPS ASSEMBLY

6 cm ($2\frac{4}{10}$″)

6 mm ($\frac{1}{4}$″) ply

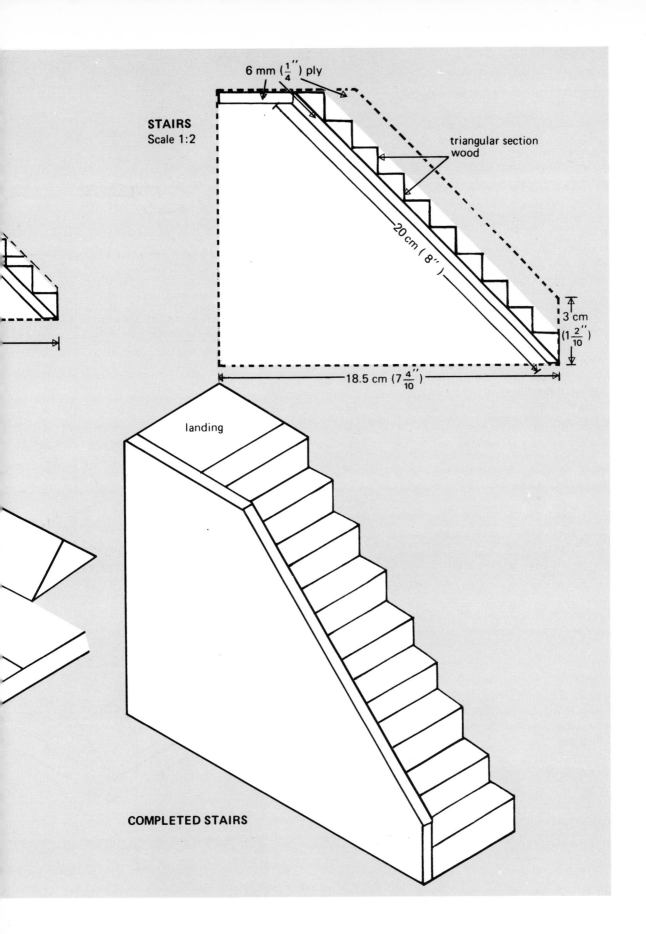

6 mm ($\frac{1}{4}''$) ply

STAIRS
Scale 1:2

triangular section wood

20 cm (8'')

3 cm ($1\frac{2}{10}''$)

18.5 cm ($7\frac{4}{10}''$)

landing

COMPLETED STAIRS

Curtains

As with wallpaper, it is essential to use either a plain material or one with a very small pattern.

Cut two strips of fabric 3×8cm ($1\frac{2}{10}'' \times 3\frac{2}{10}''$) for each window. Spread a rubber-based fabric adhesive across each curtain about 3cm ($1\frac{1}{4}''$) from the bottom. Pinch the fabric at this point so that it dries into the shape shown in the diagram.

For the pelmet (valance), cover a strip of thin card 1.5×10cm ($\frac{6}{10}'' \times 4''$) with the curtain fabric. Glue the two curtains to the back of the pelmet (valance). Glue the pelmet (valance) in place about 1cm ($\frac{4}{10}''$) above the window frame.

Furniture

Furniture for dolls houses can be purchased from toyshops, but is often expensive, poorly made and not to the correct scale. Making the furniture is fun and very inexpensive. Patterns are given full size; trace them onto thin card and use these as templates. The patterns are for a basic set of furniture. Once you start making it you will get ideas for additional pieces.

All the furniture is made from 3mm ($\frac{1}{8}''$) ply unless stated otherwise.

Kitchen chairs

Using a fretsaw, cut out the back and back legs as one piece. Cut out the heart shape. Smooth rough edges with fine sandpaper. Cut out the front legs, the area between the broken lines, and seat. Using a good quality, quick drying wood glue, stick the seat to the front legs, and then to the chair back. Make four chairs. Colour with a light wood stain, paint on flowers with gloss enamel paint, and finally cover with a coat of polyurethane varnish.

Table

Cut out the top, frame, and four legs. Glue the frame underneath the table. Glue the legs in place. Finish as the chairs.

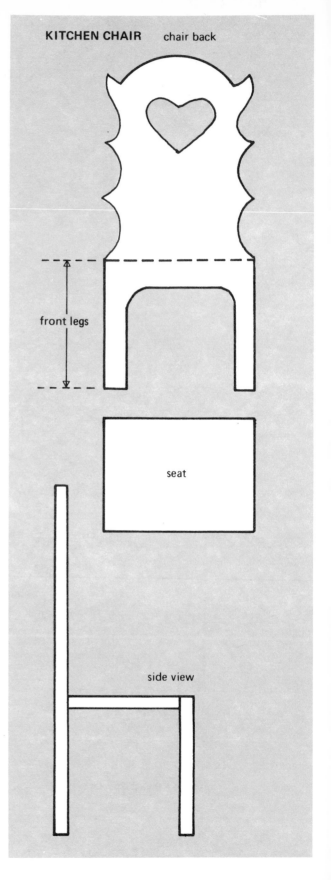

KITCHEN CHAIR   chair back

front legs

seat

side view

PELMET/VALANCE

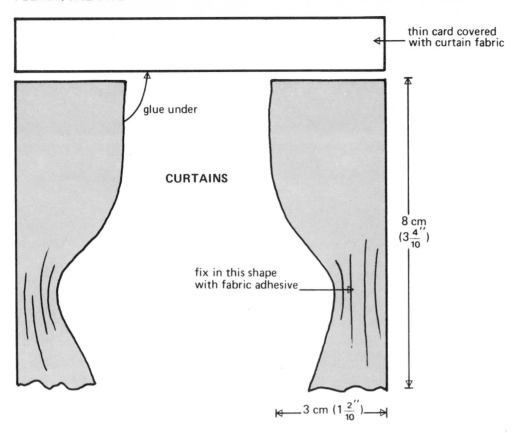

thin card covered
with curtain fabric

glue under

CURTAINS

8 cm
$(3\frac{4}{10}'')$

fix in this shape
with fabric adhesive

$\longmapsto$ 3 cm $(1\frac{2}{10}'')\longmapsto$

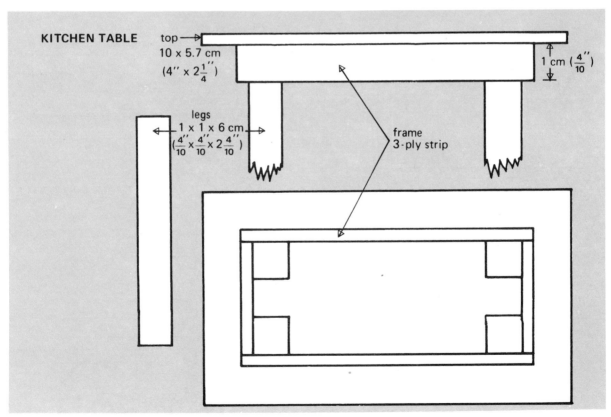

KITCHEN TABLE

top $\rightarrow$
10 x 5.7 cm
$(4'' \times 2\frac{1}{4}'')$

1 cm $(\frac{4}{10}'')$

legs
1 x 1 x 6 cm
$(\frac{4}{10}'' \times \frac{4}{10}'' \times 2\frac{4}{10}'')$

frame
3-ply strip

Dresser

Cut out the back, 2 sides, 2 shelves, top, top of base, and scalloped facing. Glue shelves, top, and top of base to sides. When dry, glue on back. Glue facing on top front. The bottom front can be left open for storage purposes, or closed in with a piece of wood; dimensions are shown on diagram.

Sitting room chairs and settle

Cut the sides of the chairs and settle from the same pattern. Cut out the seat and back for each item. Glue the seat and back to one side as shown by the broken lines in the diagram. When the glue is dry, add the other side.

Upholstery

To upholster the chairs and settle, cut a piece of thin card the size of the seat. Use this as a template to cut a piece of foam rubber 1cm ($\frac{4}{10}''$) thick. Cut a piece of fabric 1.5cm ($\frac{1}{2}''$) wider all round than the seat. Place the fabric face down on a work surface. Put foam rubber and then the card in the middle of the fabric. Put fabric adhesive on the card and pull the fabric onto it. When the glue is dry, glue the cushion to the seat. All the upholstery, the mattresses and pillows for the bed are made in the same way.

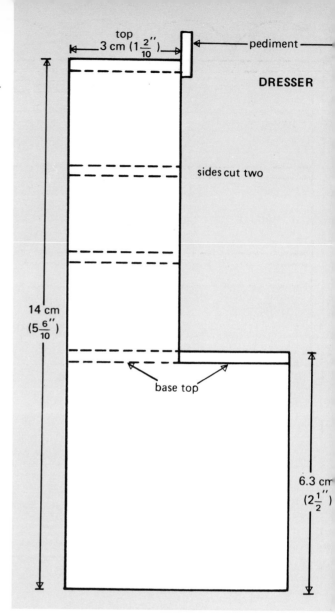

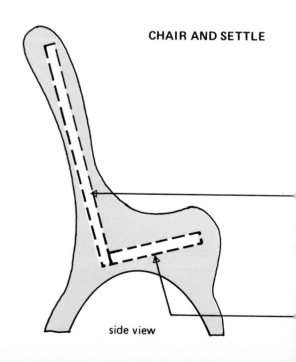

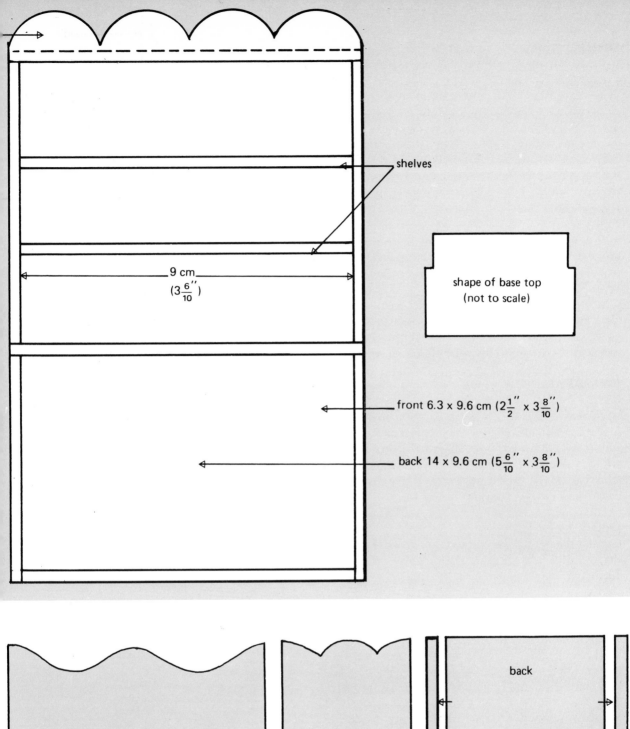

shelves

shape of base top
(not to scale)

9 cm
$(3\frac{6}{10}'')$

front 6.3 x 9.6 cm $(2\frac{1}{2}'' \times 3\frac{8}{10}'')$

back 14 x 9.6 cm $(5\frac{6}{10}'' \times 3\frac{8}{10}'')$

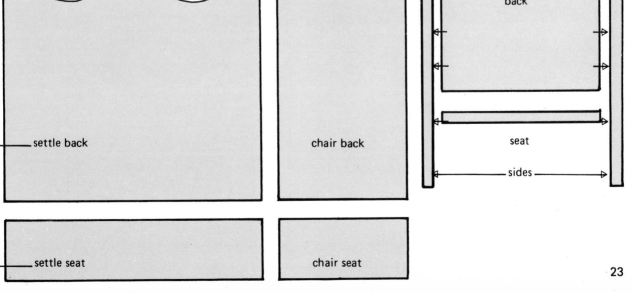

settle back

chair back

back

seat

sides

settle seat

chair seat

Dressing table

Cut out the dressing table top. Glue it to the top of a box 9cm ($3\frac{6}{10}$") across by 6cm ($2\frac{4}{10}$") deep by 8cm ($3\frac{2}{10}$") high. Make false drawer fronts by gluing two strips of ply 7 × 1.5cm ($2\frac{8}{10}$" × $\frac{6}{10}$") to the front. Make drawer pulls from very small beads. When you have painted and decorated the dressing table to match the other bedroom furniture, glue a mirror of kitchen foil backed with card to the mirror opening.

Round table

Cut out the round top. Cut out two pairs of legs, one with a 3mm ($\frac{1}{8}$") wide slot halfway down from the top, the other with a 3mm ($\frac{1}{8}$") wide slot halfway up from the bottom. Slot the legs together and glue to the top.

Give the furniture a coat of white primer, an under-coat, and two coats of white gloss paint. Paint on simple flower decorations with gloss enamel paints.

Child's bed

Cut out the head and foot pieces. Cut out a mattress base 5.5 × 12cm ($2\frac{2}{10}$" × $4\frac{8}{10}$"). Glue the mattress base to the head and foot. If extra strength is required, add sides as indicated in the diagram. Paint the bed white. Paint the figure at the head to represent a 'guardian angel'. Make a mattress and glue to the base. Make two beds for one bedroom.

Double bed

Cut out the head and foot pieces. Cut out the heart shapes in the head piece. Cut a mattress base 8.5 × 15cm ($3\frac{4}{10}$" × 6"). Assemble as the child's bed.

Chair

Cut two sides for each chair. Cut out the seat and the back. Glue the seat and back to one side as shown by the broken lines in the diagram. When the glue has set, add the other side. Make two chairs for each bedroom. Paint and upholster as described on page 22.

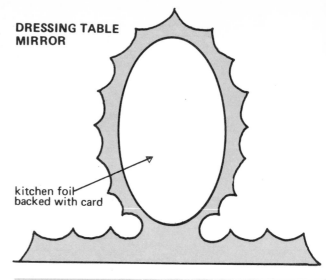

DRESSING TABLE MIRROR

kitchen foil backed with card

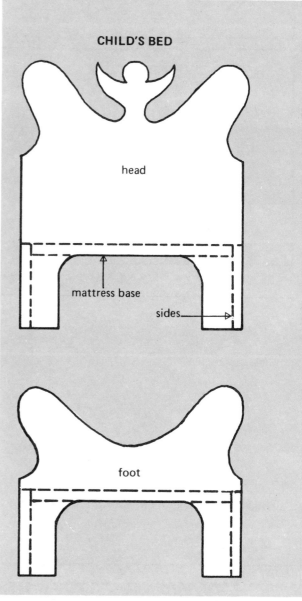

CHILD'S BED

head

mattress base

sides

foot

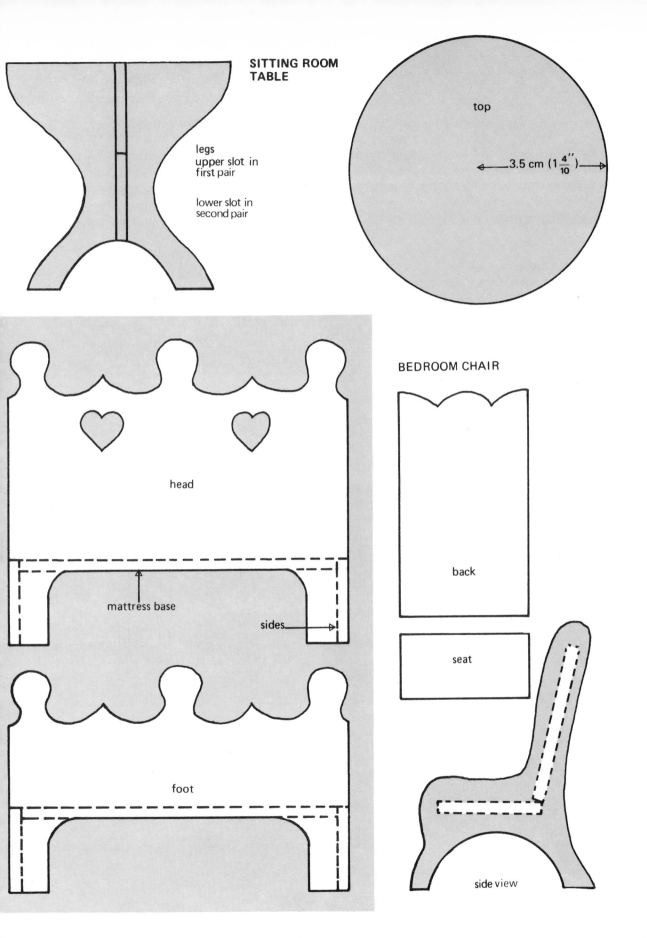

SITTING ROOM TABLE

legs
upper slot in
first pair

lower slot in
second pair

top

←— 3.5 cm ($1\frac{4}{10}''$) —→

head

mattress base

sides

foot

BEDROOM CHAIR

back

seat

side view

Bathroom

Although a separate bathroom is not included in this house, a bath, handbasin and toilet could be placed in one of the bedrooms. If desired, a movable partition wall could be made.

It is very difficult, if not impossible, to make a satisfactory bath from plywood using the tools normally available. It is best to look around in toyshops to find a plastic bath, handbasin and toilet. Try to get them to the same scale as the other Chalet furniture (1:12).

Bathroom stool

The bathroom stool shown here is simple to make and looks attractive with its neat cork seat.

Cut out two pairs of legs and two side pieces. Glue the four pieces together to form base of stool. Cut cork seat from floor tile or table mat. Glue on top of stool base. Paint legs white and give cork seat two or three coats of polyurethane varnish.

Kitchen stove

The kitchen stove shown opposite is made from five pieces of wood glued together.

Cut out back, two sides, front and top. Glue sides to back. Glue on front. Cut short length of 3mm ($\frac{1}{8}$″) square balsa wood (you should have some left over from making the window frames) for handle, and glue on oven door. Glue on top. After painting, stick on card circles to represent hotplates or burners and switches.

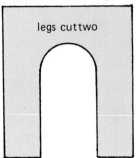

BATHROOM STOOL

legs cut two

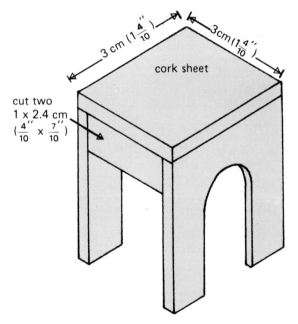

3 cm (1 $\frac{4}{10}$″)

3 cm (1 $\frac{4}{10}$″)

cork sheet

cut two
1 x 2.4 cm
($\frac{4}{10}$″ x $\frac{7}{10}$″)

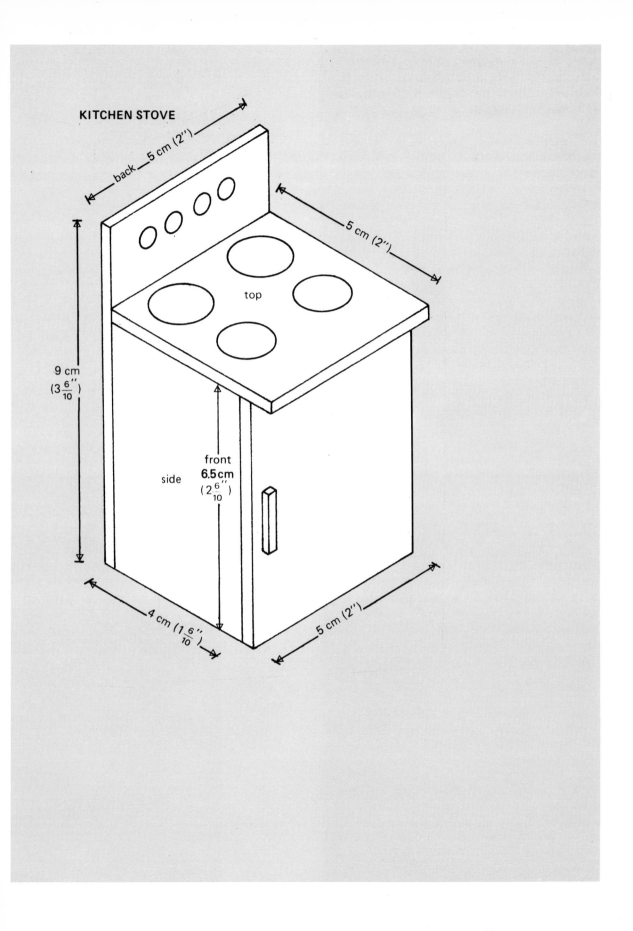

KITCHEN STOVE

back — 5 cm (2")

5 cm (2")

top

9 cm $(3\frac{6}{10}'')$

front
6.5 cm
$(2\frac{6}{10}'')$

side

4 cm $(1\frac{6}{10}'')$

5 cm (2")

Washing machine

This is a simple box structure. Cut out front, back, two sides and top. Smooth rough edges, then glue sides to back and front. When glue has set, glue on top. Make switches and dials from card and glue to front.

Refrigerator

You can make a refrigerator using the same structure as the washing machine, or adapting it to a taller shape.

Sink unit

Cut out two sides, back and front. Glue together. Cut out one sink side, and sink bottom 4×4cm ($1\frac{6}{10}'' \times 1\frac{6}{10}''$). Cut out sink top, cutting out inner square along solid line (broken lines are guides for gluing top to unit). Cut out sink side 4×2.5cm ($1\frac{6}{10}'' \times 1''$) and glue in place between front and back, flush with top edges. Next glue sink bottom in place. Finally, glue sink top in place.

Paint main part of unit white. Paint sink and drainer with silver paint to represent stainless steel.

WASHING MACHINE

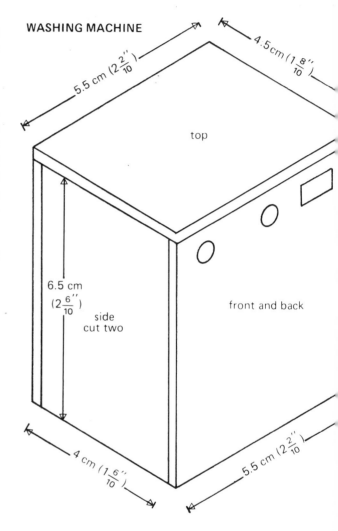

5.5 cm ($2\frac{2}{10}''$)

4.5 cm ($1\frac{8}{10}''$)

top

6.5 cm ($2\frac{6}{10}''$)

side
cut two

front and back

4 cm ($1\frac{6}{10}''$)

5.5 cm ($2\frac{2}{10}''$)

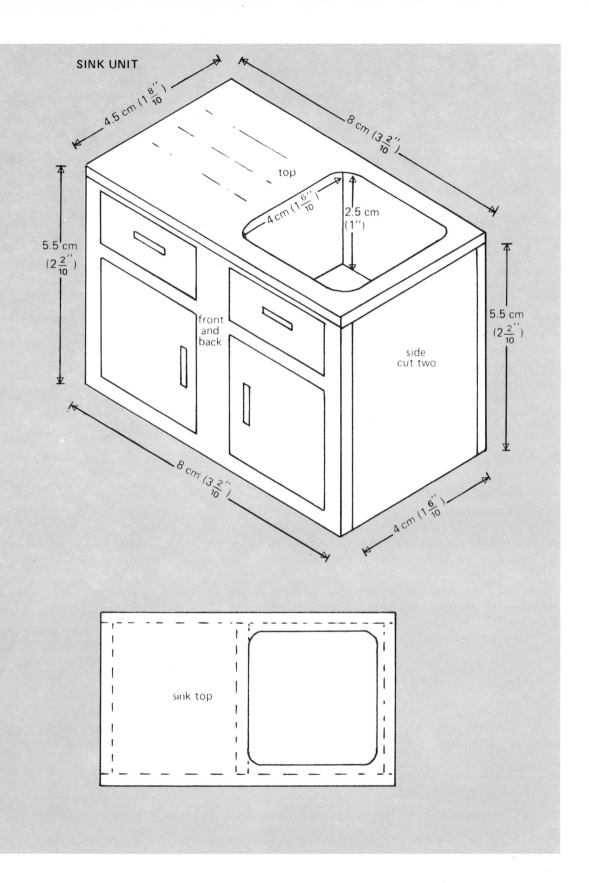

SINK UNIT

4.5 cm (1 $\frac{8}{10}$ ″)

8 cm (3 $\frac{2}{10}$ ″)

top

4 cm (1 $\frac{6}{10}$ ″)

2.5 cm (1″)

5.5 cm (2 $\frac{2}{10}$ ″)

front and back

side cut two

5.5 cm (2 $\frac{2}{10}$ ″)

8 cm (3 $\frac{2}{10}$ ″)

4 cm (1 $\frac{6}{10}$ ″)

sink top

THE MODERN BUNGALOW

The patio, made of a frame of spars and cross spars fixed to a base, is situated in front of the sliding doors.

The word bungalow comes from the Hindi *bangla*, meaning 'from Bengal'. The dictionary defines a bungalow as 'a one-storey building originally lightly built or temporary'. From this definition it would be reasonable to say that the bungalow must be one of the oldest types of house.

From the builder's point of view the bungalow is much cheaper to build than a two- or three-storey house. Because it is only one storey the foundations do not need to be as deep or as strong as those needed to support a multistorey building. The walls have to support only the roof, so they do not need to be as thick as those in a multistorey house. The lintels over the door and window·openings can be of much lighter construction and a staircase is not needed.

To counter the cheapness of building, however, the bungalow, with its rooms all on ground level and its garden, covers more land. For this reason bungalows have been built in those areas where land prices are relatively low, or where the underlying rock is not capable of supporting heavier buildings. On the outskirts of many large towns and cities there are large estates composed entirely of bungalows, though some of these buildings may have extra rooms built immediately under the roof, with light entering through dormer windows.

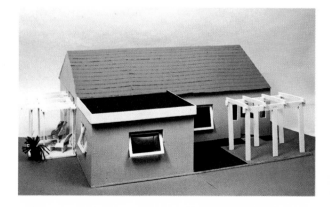

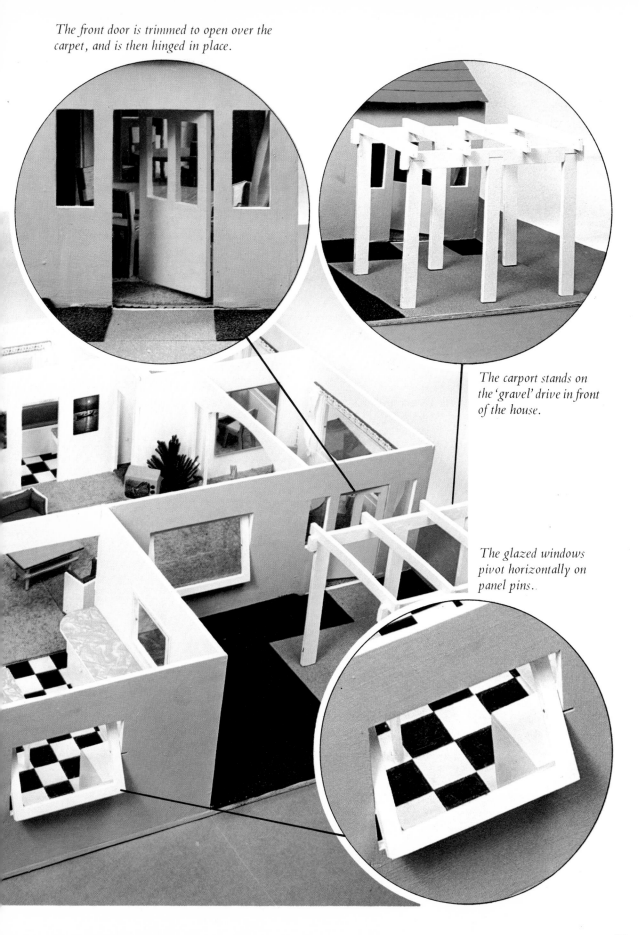

The front door is trimmed to open over the carpet, and is then hinged in place.

The carport stands on the 'gravel' drive in front of the house.

The glazed windows pivot horizontally on panel pins.

Building the bungalow

Materials

1 sheet 6mm ($\frac{1}{4}''$) plywood 240×120cm ($8' \times 4'$)
1 sheet 3mm ($\frac{1}{8}''$) plywood 120×120cm ($4' \times 4'$)
2 sheets thick card 64×52cm ($26'' \times 21''$)
2 sheets thin white card 64×52cm ($26'' \times 21''$)
1 sheet thin black card 64×52cm ($26'' \times 21''$)
2 2.5cm ($1''$) brass hinges and screws to fit
1.2cm ($\frac{1}{2}''$) and 1.8cm ($\frac{3}{4}''$) panel pins
1m ($3'$) 6mm ($\frac{1}{4}''$) dowel rod
1m ($3'$) 6mm ($\frac{1}{4}''$) square balsa wood
1 polystyrene ceiling tile 30cm ($12''$) square
4 sheets coarse sandpaper
clear acetate sheet
woodworking glue and fabric adhesive
fabric, foam rubber, clear and patterned self-adhesive
  vinyl, paint

The basic structure

Cut out base 85cm ($34''$) square from 6mm ($\frac{1}{4}''$) plywood. All walls are fixed onto base.

Mark out seven exterior walls as shown opposite. When marking out window openings, also mark out window frames 1cm ($\frac{4}{10}''$) wide all round.

Check measurements and then cut out walls. Cut out waste wood from inside window frames, and then carefully cut round outer edge of frames. Mark each frame and opening so that you know where each frame fits.

Fitting window frames

Hinge frames in window openings. Each frame pivots on two 1.8cm ($\frac{3}{4}''$) panel pins that pass through centre of frame into wall. Use a fine drill to make holes in frame, push panel pin through holes, fit frame in opening, and gently tap pin into wall with light hammer. Check that frame pivots easily; use sandpaper and sharp craft knife to trim frame and opening to get good fit. Gently ease out panel pins and remove frames for painting and glazing. Give frames two coats of emulsion paint. Cut acetate sheet slightly smaller than frame and glue inside frame. Refit frames after decorating house.

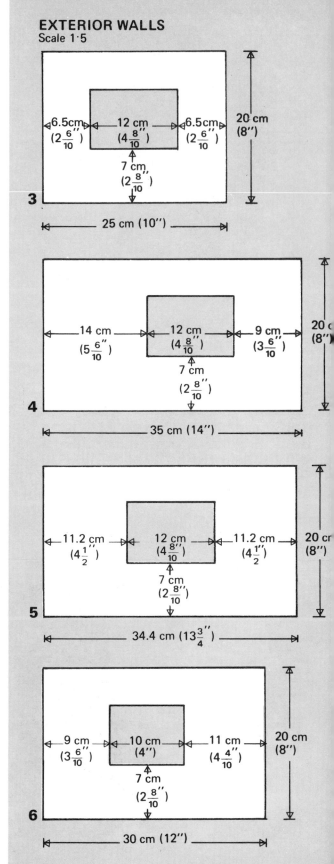

EXTERIOR WALLS
Scale 1·5

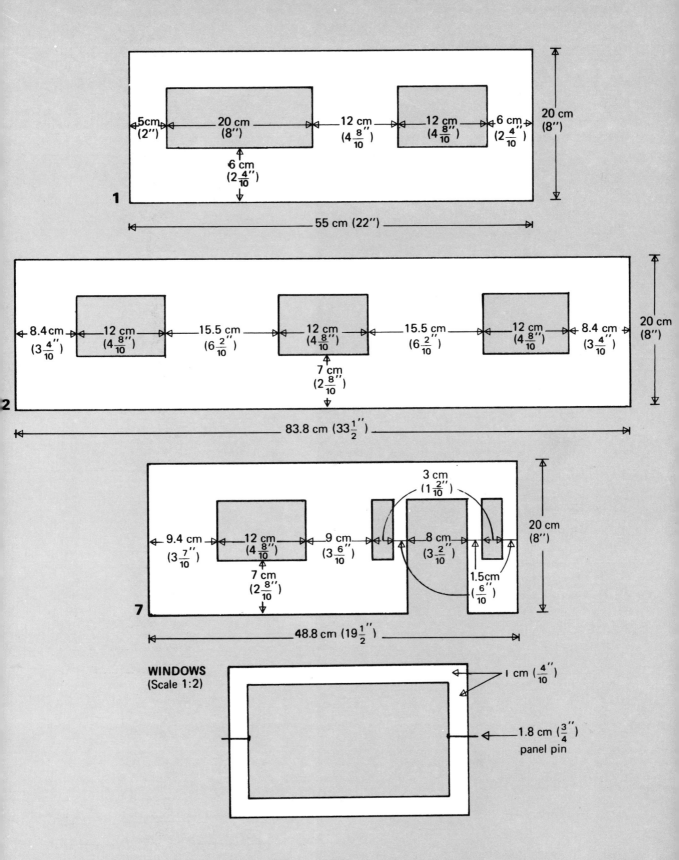

1

5 cm (2")

20 cm (8")

12 cm (4 8/10")

12 cm (4 8/10")

6 cm (2 4/10")

20 cm (8")

6 cm (2 4/10")

55 cm (22")

2

8.4 cm (3 4/10")

12 cm (4 8/10")

15.5 cm (6 2/10")

12 cm (4 8/10")

15.5 cm (6 2/10")

12 cm (4 8/10")

8.4 cm (3 4/10")

20 cm (8")

7 cm (2 8/10")

83.8 cm (33 1/2")

7

9.4 cm (3 7/10")

12 cm (4 8/10")

9 cm (3 6/10")

3 cm (1 2/10")

8 cm (3 2/10")

20 cm (8")

7 cm (2 8/10")

1.5 cm (6/10")

48.8 cm (19 1/2")

WINDOWS
(Scale 1:2)

1 cm (4/10")

1.8 cm (3/4")
panel pin

33

Assembling exterior walls

Glue and pin exterior walls to base, using 1.2cm ($\frac{1}{2}''$) panel pins. Draw guide lines under base to help in positioning panel pins. Look carefully at ground plan to see how walls are pinned to each other. The gap between walls at rear of house is filled later by sliding doors.

Interior walls

Cut out interior walls. To draw arch in wall across living/dining area (A) near front door, use a pair of compasses. Put compass point midway along bottom edge of wall and set compasses at 18cm ($7\frac{2}{10}''$) radius.

Pin and glue walls B to E, and C to F first. Glue and pin these to base and to exterior walls. Fit wall D. Next fit wall A. Finally, glue strip of wood G flush with tops of kitchen walls; it gives walls added strength.

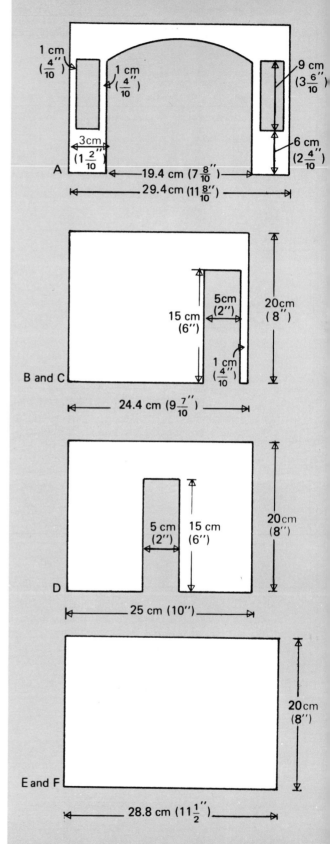

INTERIOR WALLS

GROUND PLAN

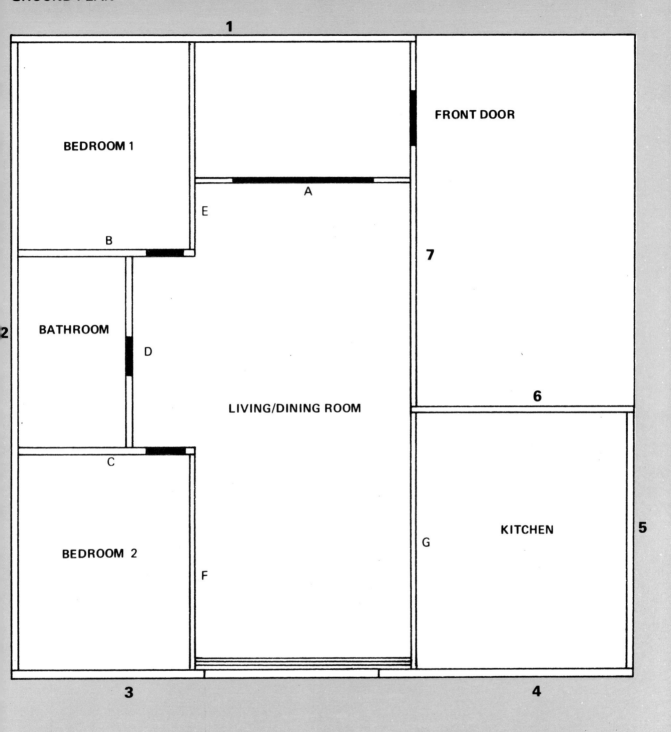

1

BEDROOM 1

FRONT DOOR

A

E

B

7

2

BATHROOM

D

LIVING/DINING ROOM

6

C

KITCHEN

5

BEDROOM 2

F

G

3

4

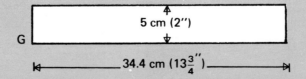

G

5 cm (2″)

34.4 cm (13$\frac{3}{4}$″)

Main roof

From 6mm ($\frac{1}{4}''$) plywood cut out main roof 85 × 55cm (34″ × 22″). Before cutting check that it will cover all rooms except kitchen. Cut out four roof supports. Glue and pin supports to roof. To give supports extra strength, glue small blocks of waste wood to angle between roof support and roof.

To keep roof lightweight cover it with thick cardboard instead of plywood. The cardboard should fit flush with end roof supports and with two long edges.

Roof tiles

Draw tiles on strips of card to dimensions shown opposite. Cut along solid lines between tiles. Fix first layer of tiles just overlapping eaves. Glue next layer in place so that tiles alternate. To make ridge tile fold strip of card 5 × 85cm (2″ × 34″) in half lengthways. Glue on ridge tile. Paint underside of roof (ceiling) white and tiles red. Trim tiles flush with roof where it joins kitchen roof.

Kitchen roof

Cut kitchen roof 35.6 × 30cm (14$\frac{1}{4}''$ × 12″) from 6mm ($\frac{1}{4}''$) plywood. Glue strips of 6mm ($\frac{1}{4}''$) ply to top on all four sides. To make outer frame glue strips of 3mm ($\frac{1}{8}''$) ply 3cm (1$\frac{1}{4}''$) wide to three external edges (see diagram). Cover rooftop with coarse sandpaper and paint with matt black paint. Paint underside of roof (ceiling) and outer frame white.

Front door

Cut out front door. Fit in place after decorating house.

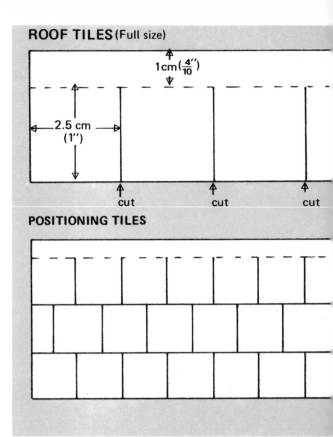

ROOF TILES (Full size)

1cm ($\frac{4}{10}''$)

2.5 cm (1″)

cut   cut   cut

POSITIONING TILES

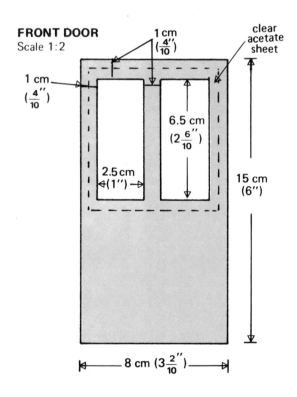

FRONT DOOR
Scale 1:2

1 cm ($\frac{4}{10}''$)

clear acetate sheet

1 cm ($\frac{4}{10}''$)

6.5 cm (2$\frac{6}{10}''$)

2.5 cm (1″)

15 cm (6″)

8 cm (3$\frac{2}{10}''$)

MAIN ROOF (Scale 1:5)

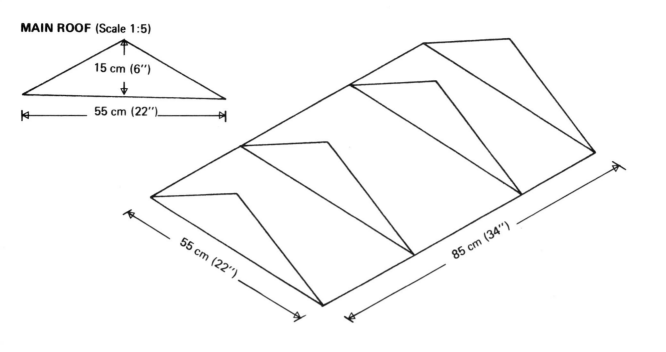

15 cm (6")

55 cm (22")

55 cm (22")

85 cm (34")

KITCHEN ROOF

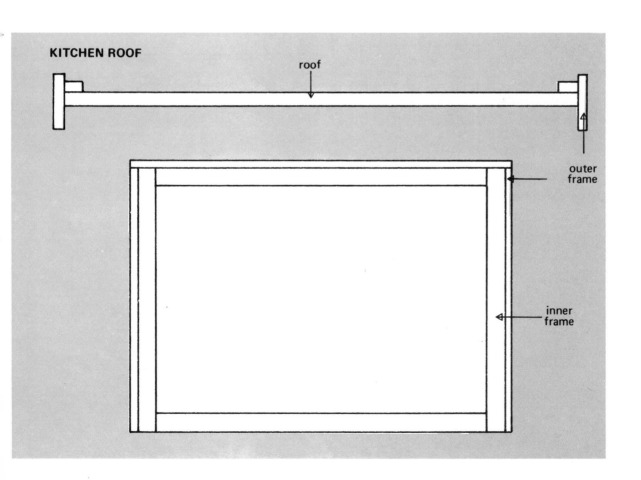

roof

outer frame

inner frame

Patio doors

The doors are made up with grooved sections as a unit. The unit is glued in place behind opening between walls 3 and 4.

Cut door frames from 3mm ($\frac{1}{8}''$) ply. Although measurements are given on drawings, it is best to make sliding doors to measurements taken from your own bungalow. You may find that minor inaccuracies will cause you to alter these measurements slightly.

To make upper and lower grooved sections pin and glue 3 strips of 3mm ($\frac{1}{8}''$) square balsa wood to strips of 6mm ($\frac{1}{4}''$) ply 28.8 × 1.7cm ($11\frac{1}{2}'' \times \frac{3}{4}''$).

Remove balsa for 6mm ($\frac{1}{4}''$) at both ends of upper and lower grooved sections so that upright frame ends can be pinned in place. Cut strips of 6mm ($\frac{1}{4}''$) ply 18.8cm ($7\frac{1}{2}''$) long for frame ends. Pin between upper and lower grooved sections at each end to make frame. Insert doors to complete unit, making sure they slide easily in grooves. Take unit apart and paint all parts white. To glaze doors glue acetate sheet to back. Fit doors back into grooves, and glue and pin grooved sections to frame ends. Glue unit to base and walls 3 and 4.

Patio

Cut out base to dimensions shown, using 6mm ($\frac{1}{4}''$) ply. Cut out spars C and D. They are held above base by six 6mm ($\frac{1}{4}''$) dowel rods 18cm ($7\frac{2}{10}''$) long. Find drill bit that will cut holes in which dowel rod is tight fit. Mark hole centres on base 1cm ($\frac{4}{10}''$) from each edge. Clamp spars C and D under base one at a time, and drill holes through base and spar. Cut dowel rods and glue into holes in base. Fit spars on top.

Cut cross spars A and B. Mark .exact position of notches in these spars from your own construction. Glue spars A and B in place. Paint patio white.

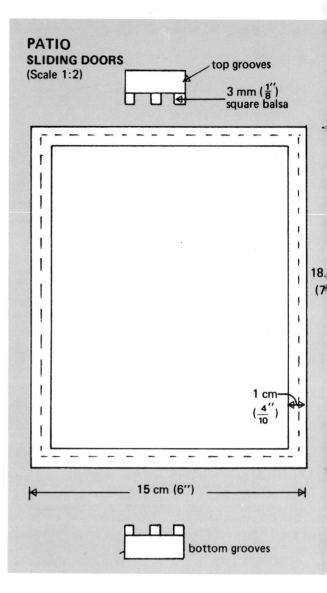

PATIO SLIDING DOORS (Scale 1:2)

top grooves

3 mm ($\frac{1}{8}''$) square balsa

18. (7

15 cm (6'')

1 cm ($\frac{4}{10}''$)

bottom grooves

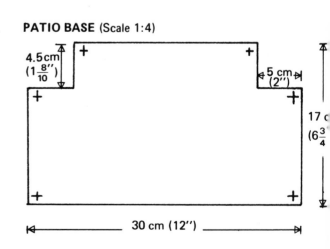

PATIO BASE (Scale 1:4)

4.5cm ($1\frac{8}{10}''$)

5 cm (2'')

17 c ($6\frac{3}{4}$

30 cm (12'')

SPARS (Scale 1:2)

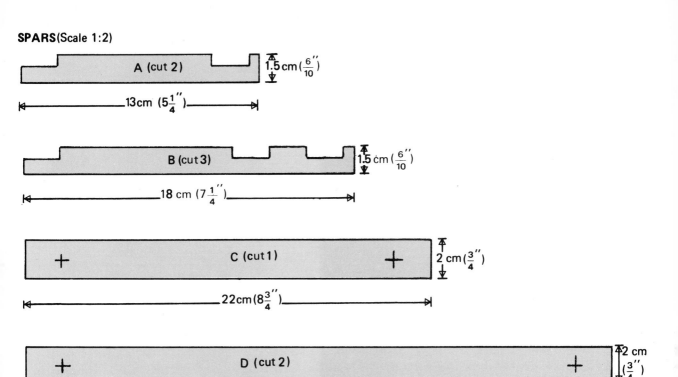

A (cut 2)   1.5 cm ($\frac{6''}{10}$)

13cm ($5\frac{1}{4}''$)

B (cut 3)   1.5 cm ($\frac{6''}{10}$)

18 cm ($7\frac{1}{4}''$)

C (cut 1)   2 cm ($\frac{3''}{4}$)

22cm ($8\frac{3}{4}''$)

D (cut 2)   2 cm ($\frac{3''}{4}$)

32 cm ($12\frac{3}{4}''$)

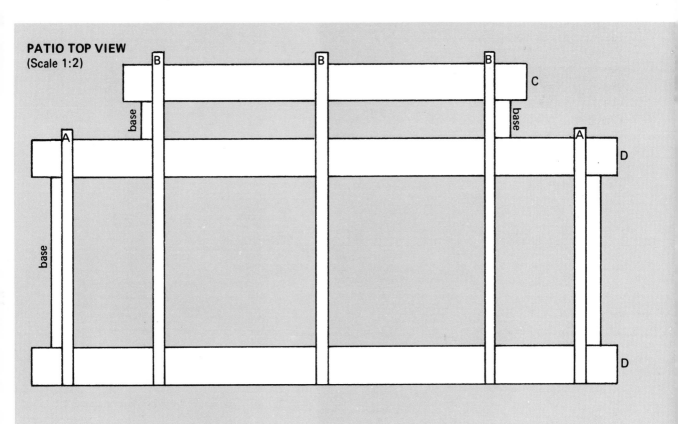

PATIO TOP VIEW
(Scale 1:2)

B   B   B

C

base   base

A   A

D

base

D

Decoration

Paint or paper all interior walls. If walls are being papered, follow instructions given in **Before you begin . . .** (page 9).

Tile kitchen and bathroom floors with 3cm ($1\frac{1}{4}''$) squares of black and white card. Cut tiles accurately and cover with clear self-adhesive vinyl. Cover bedrooms and living/dining area floors with 30cm (12″) square carpet tiles. When these have been fitted, trim bottom of front door so that when hinged in place it will open over carpet. Use two 2.5cm (1″) brass hinges to hinge front door. Remove door, paint, glaze window with clear acetate sheet, and refit.

Curtains

Cut suitable fabric into pieces 6×14cm ($2\frac{4}{10}'' \times 5\frac{6}{10}''$). Use fabric adhesive to make hems top and bottom. Pleat fabric top and bottom, fixing pleats in place with fabric adhesive. Make pelmets (valances) from 6mm ($\frac{1}{4}''$) square balsa wood 4cm ($1\frac{6}{10}''$) longer than window openings. Glue pair of curtains to each pelmet (valance) and glue in place just above windows. Now fix windows in place.

Garden

Cut flower bed from polystyrene ceiling tile. Paint brown and glue in place. Use coarse sandpaper to represent gravel. Grass can be either grass paper from a model-making shop, or simply painted. Make flowers for garden from tissue paper and wire (see pages 72–73).

Carport

Cut out two sides and four top spars from 6mm ($\frac{1}{4}''$) ply. Cut notches in spars 5mm ($\frac{1}{4}''$) deep and as wide as sides are thick. Glue spars to sides. Paint white. Place on gravel in garden.

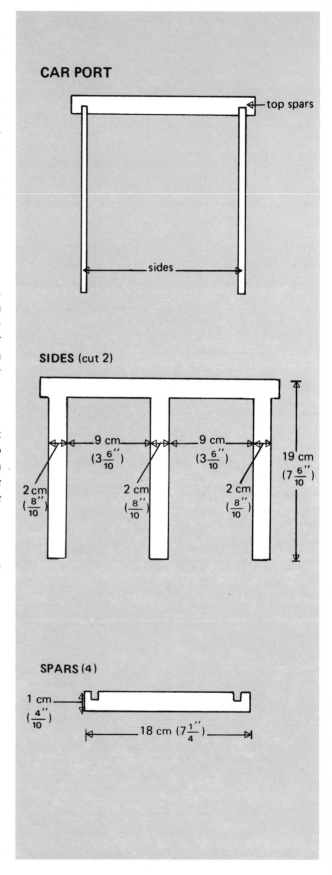

CAR PORT

top spars

sides

SIDES (cut 2)

9 cm ($3\frac{6}{10}''$)   9 cm ($3\frac{6}{10}''$)   19 cm ($7\frac{6}{10}''$)

2 cm ($\frac{8}{10}''$)   2 cm ($\frac{8}{10}''$)   2 cm ($\frac{8}{10}''$)

SPARS (4)

1 cm ($\frac{4}{10}''$)

18 cm ($7\frac{1}{4}''$)

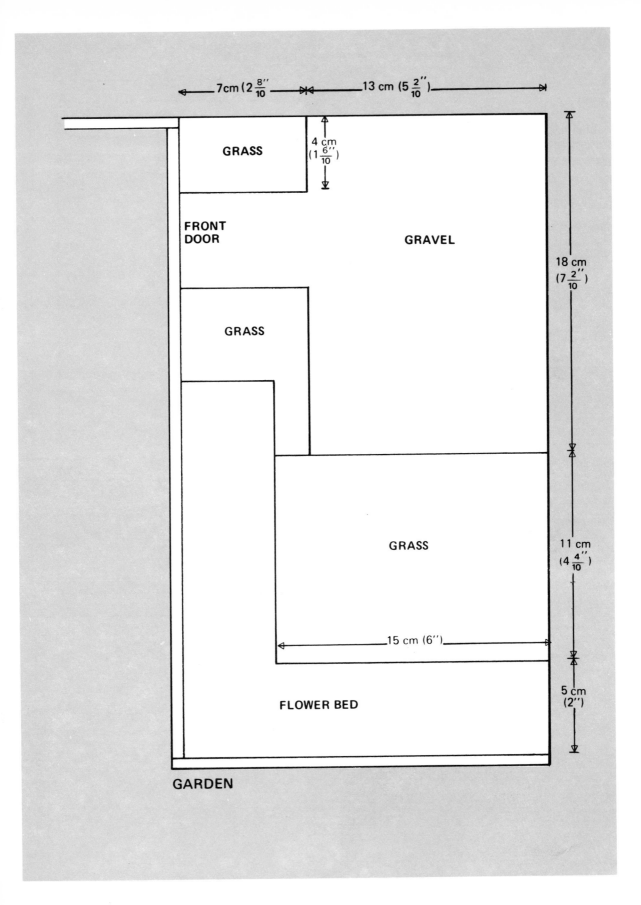

7cm (2 8/10") — 13 cm (5 2/10")

GRASS

4 cm (1 6/10")

FRONT DOOR

GRAVEL

18 cm (7 2/10")

GRASS

GRASS

11 cm (4 4/10")

15 cm (6")

FLOWER BED

5 cm (2")

GARDEN

Furniture

All furniture is made from 3mm ($\frac{1}{8}''$) plywood and patterns are given full size unless stated otherwise. Trace patterns onto thin card and use these as templates.

Kitchen table

Cut out top and drill four holes for legs. Cut four legs from 6mm ($\frac{1}{4}''$) dowel. After smoothing down rough edges, glue legs in place. Cover table top with self-adhesive vinyl.

Washing machine

Cut out two sides, back and front. Glue pieces together to form open-ended box. Glue on top. When glue is dry, round off top front edge with sandpaper. Paint. Stick on black card circles for switches and circle of kitchen foil for front window.

Cupboard unit

This pattern is given half size.

Cut out top and front from 3mm ($\frac{1}{8}''$) ply. Cut shelf same size as part of top left of broken lines in drawing. Cut two ends 5.7×6cm ($2\frac{2}{10}'' \times 2\frac{4}{10}''$) from 6mm ($\frac{1}{4}''$) plywood. Glue and pin top and front to ends. Glue shelf in place. Glue on drawer fronts cut from 3mm ($\frac{1}{8}''$) ply. Make handles from scraps of wood or card. Paint front and sides, then cover top with self-adhesive vinyl as used for table.

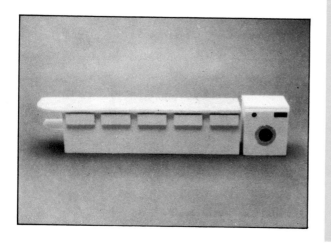

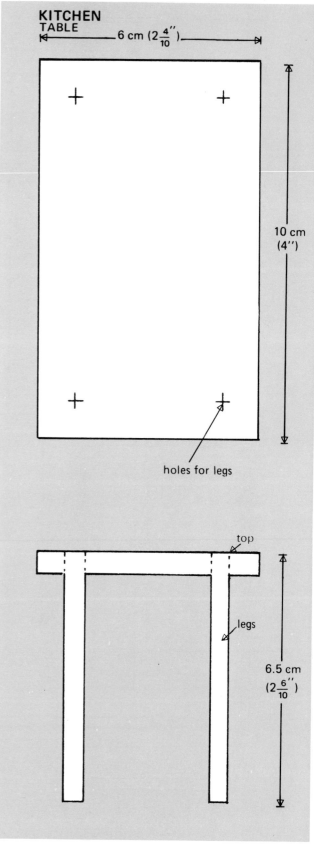

KITCHEN TABLE

6 cm ($2\frac{4}{10}''$)

10 cm (4'')

holes for legs

top

legs

6.5 cm ($2\frac{6}{10}''$)

CUPBOARD UNIT (Scale 1:2)

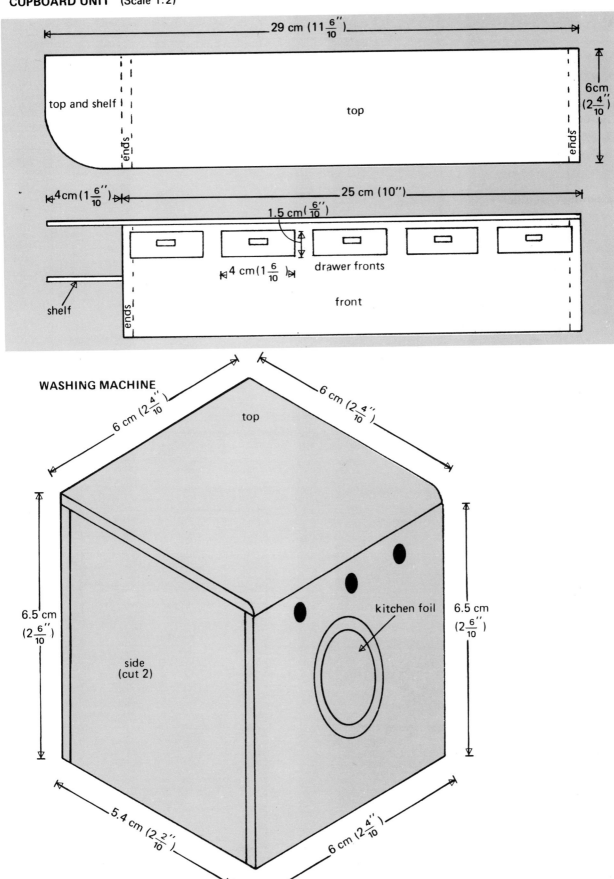

29 cm (11 6/10")

top and shelf

top

ends

6cm (2 4/10")

4cm (1 6/10")

25 cm (10")

1.5 cm (6/10")

4 cm (1 6/10")

drawer fronts

shelf

ends

front

WASHING MACHINE

6 cm (2 4/10")

6 cm (2 4/10")

top

6.5 cm (2 6/10")

6.5 cm (2 6/10")

kitchen foil

side (cut 2)

5.4 cm (2 2/10")

6 cm (2 4/10")

Refrigerator

The sizes of the parts are shown in the small drawing on page 45. Cut out sides, back and front (shown full size). Glue together, then cut top to fit. Glue on top and two handles. Paint.

Kitchen stove

The sizes of the parts are shown in the small drawing on page 45. The front view is shown full size. Cut out back, front, and two sides. Glue sides between back and front. Cut out top and fix in place. After painting, glue black card circles to top to represent burners. Glue small black card circles to back to represent switches.

Sink unit

Cut out top, front, and two sides 6×5.4cm ($2\frac{4}{10}'' \times 2\frac{2}{10}''$). Glue together. Fix side of sink 5.4×2cm ($2\frac{2}{10}'' \times \frac{8}{10}''$) in place. Glue on bottom 7.5×5.4cm ($3'' \times 2\frac{2}{10}''$), and then back of unit. Paint.

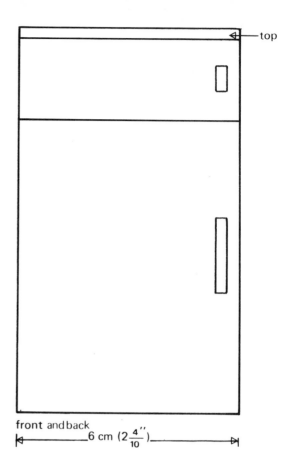

front and back
6 cm ($2\frac{4}{10}''$)

KITCHEN STOVE

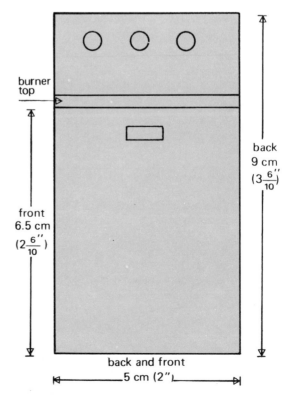

burner top

back 9 cm ($3\frac{6}{10}''$)

front 6.5 cm ($2\frac{6}{10}''$)

back and front
5 cm (2")

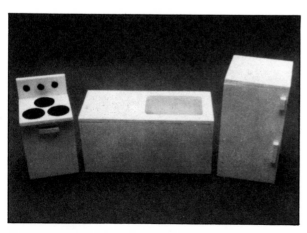

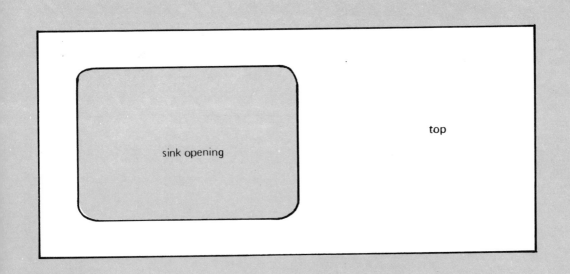

SINK UNIT

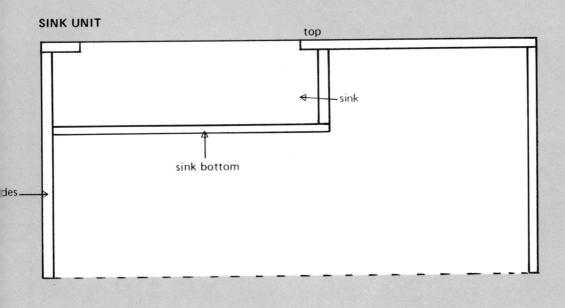

top

sink

sink bottom

des

KITCHEN STOVE
SIDE VIEW

Scale 1:2

REFRIGERATOR SIDE VIEW

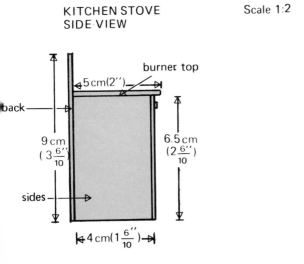

burner top

5 cm(2'')

back

9 cm
(3 $\frac{6}{10}$'')

6.5 cm
(2 $\frac{6}{10}$'')

sides

4 cm(1 $\frac{6}{10}$'')

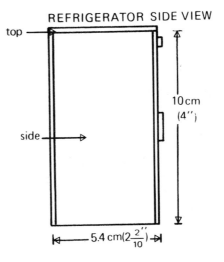

top

side

10 cm
(4'')

5.4 cm(2 $\frac{2}{10}$'')

Dining table

Cut out top, two circles A and one circle B. Drill holes through centres of A and B so that 6mm ($\frac{1}{4}$″) dowel is tight fit. Cut 4cm ($1\frac{6}{10}$″) length of dowel and glue into hole in one circle A. Glue circle B on top of A. Glue other circle A to other end of dowel. Glue on top. Check that table is straight before glue sets. Stain and varnish.

Dining table chairs

Make four chairs. For each chair cut out two sides, back and seat. Smooth down rough edges and glue seats and backs to sides. Stain and varnish.

Sideboard

Cut out front, back, top and two sides. Glue front and back to sides. Glue on top. Stain and varnish.

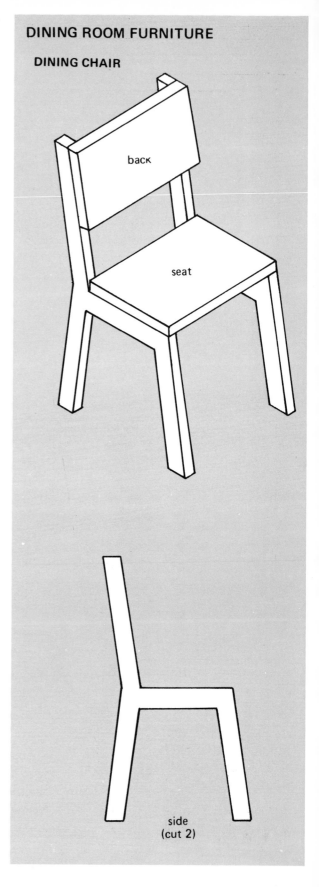

DINING ROOM FURNITURE

DINING CHAIR

back

seat

side
(cut 2)

TABLE

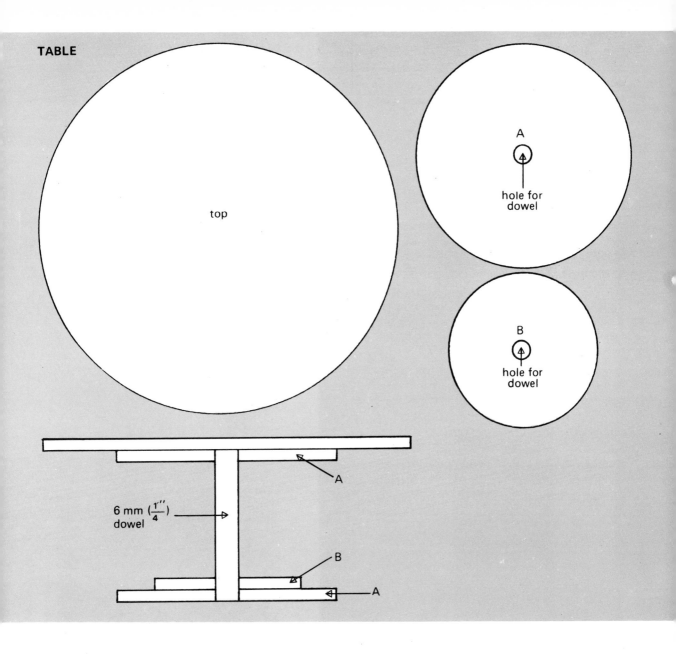

top

A

hole for
dowel

B

hole for
dowel

6 mm ($\frac{1''}{4}$)
dowel

A

B

A

SIDEBOARD

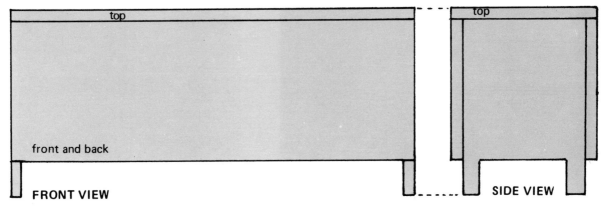

top

top

front and back

FRONT VIEW

SIDE VIEW

Living room armchairs and settee

Cut out six sides. Cut out backs, fronts and seats for armchairs and settee. For armchairs, glue back to two sides. Glue front in place, and then seat. Glue parts of settee together in same order. Paint white.

Upholstery

To upholster chairs and settee, cut pieces of card slightly smaller than seat back and sides. Use these as templates to cut pieces of foam rubber 1cm ($\frac{4}{10}$") thick. Cut fabric 1.5cm ($\frac{1}{2}$") wider all round than piece of card. Place fabric face down on work surface. Put foam rubber and then card in middle of fabric. Put fabric adhesive on card, and pull fabric onto it. Finish corners neatly, as though wrapping up a parcel. Glue cushions to chairs and settee.

Television

Cut out top, base, front, back and two sides. Drill four holes in base to take 6mm ($\frac{1}{4}$") dowel. Cut four legs 3cm ($1\frac{2}{10}$") long from dowel. Glue legs in place splaying outwards slightly. Glue front and sides to base. Glue on top and back. Stain and varnish. Cut out picture from a magazine and glue to front to represent screen. Make small black card circles to represent control knobs.

Coffee table

Cut out top and shelves. Mark in centres for holes on shelves. Drill through both shelves together. Cut legs from 6mm ($\frac{1}{4}$") dowel. Glue legs flush with top of shelf A. Glue shelf B about 1cm ($\frac{1}{2}$") down from A. Glue top in place. Stain and varnish.

LIVING ROOM FURNITURE

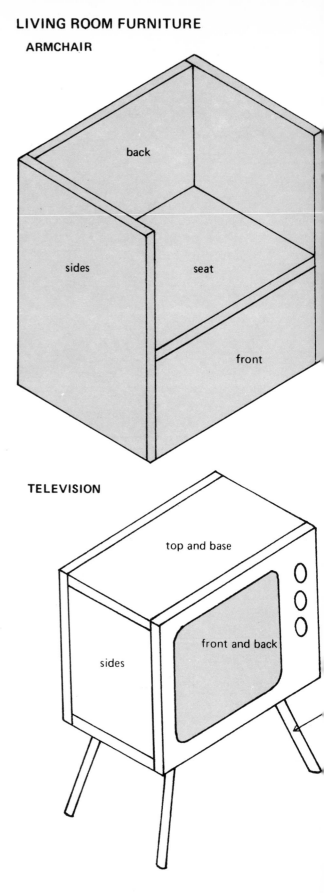

ARMCHAIR

back

sides

seat

front

TELEVISION

top and base

front and back

sides

SETTEE

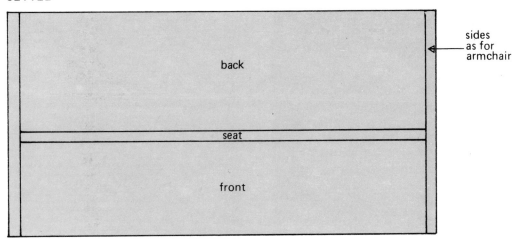

back

seat

front

sides
as for
armchair

COFFEE TABLE

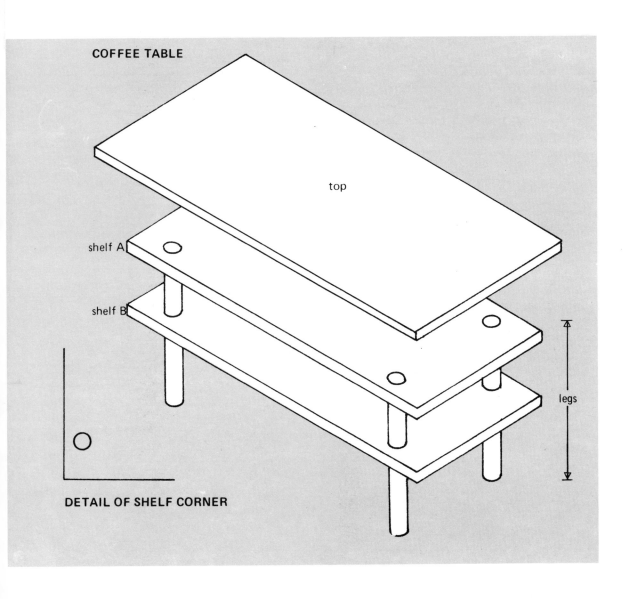

top

shelf A

shelf B

legs

DETAIL OF SHELF CORNER

Dressing table

Cut out top. Drill three holes for mirror supports equally spaced between sides. Cut out three oval mirrors. Cut three dowel supports 3cm ($1\frac{2}{10}''$) long. Cut dowel down length for 1.5cm ($\frac{1}{2}''$) to make flat surface to glue to backs of mirrors.

Cut out back and two sides 5.5 × 3.5cm ($2\frac{2}{10}''$ × $1\frac{4}{10}''$). Glue sides to back, then fix top in place. Glue mirror supports in place, or leave so that mirrors can swivel. Paint, then cover mirror fronts with kitchen foil. To complete, glue fabric curtain along front edge of top.

Wardrobe

Cut out front, back, two sides 15 × 5cm (6″ × 2″) and top 14.4 × 5cm ($5\frac{3}{4}''$ × 2″). Glue sides and top to back. Fix front in place. Cut door fronts and handles from thin card, and glue on. Paint.

Make two wardrobes and two dressing tables.

Bedroom chest of drawers

Cut out back, front, two sides 5.5 × 4cm ($2\frac{2}{10}''$ × $1\frac{6}{10}''$), and top 8 × 4.6cm ($3\frac{2}{10}''$ × $1\frac{8}{10}''$). Glue pieces together to form box. Cut drawer fronts and handles from card and glue on. Paint.

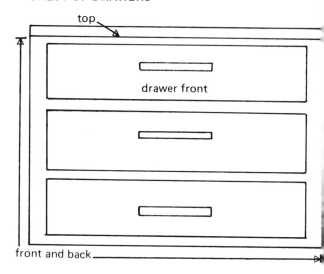

CHEST OF DRAWERS

top

drawer front

front and back

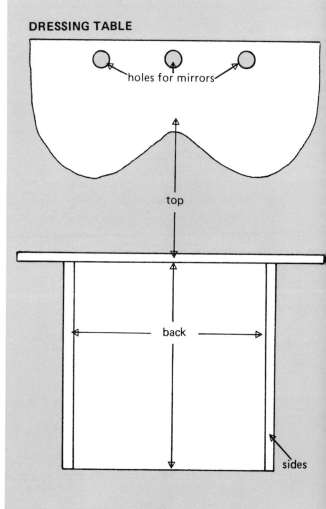

DRESSING TABLE

holes for mirrors

top

back

sides

WARDROBE

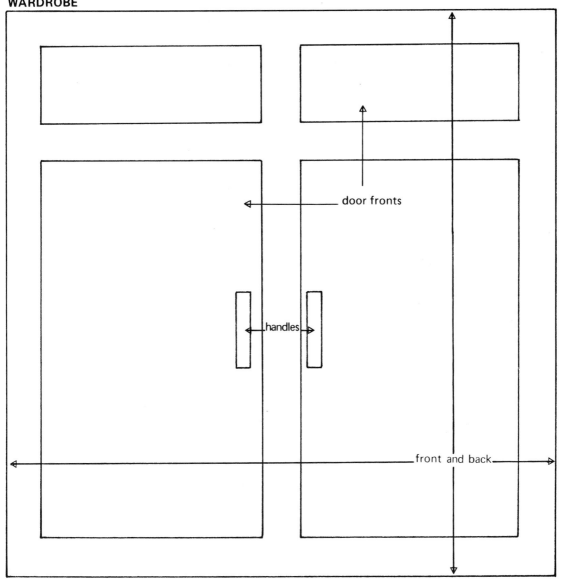

door fronts

handles

front and back

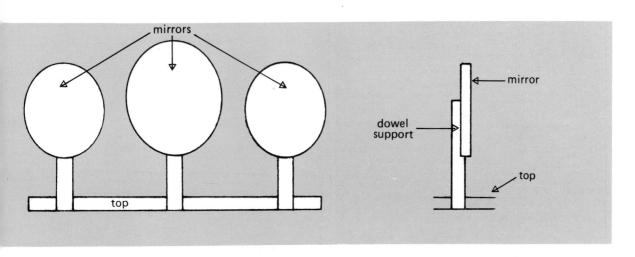

mirrors

top

mirror

dowel
support

top

Single bed

Cut head 5×6cm ($2'' \times 2\frac{4}{10}''$), foot 2×6cm ($\frac{8}{10}'' \times 2\frac{4}{10}''$), and base 10×6cm ($4'' \times 2\frac{4}{10}''$). Glue together and paint. Make mattress and pillow using method described for upholstering armchairs and settee.

Double bed

Cut out headboard, foot, base, two sides and two shelves. Glue sides to foot. Glue base on top. Fix this unit to centre of headboard. Glue shelves in place 4cm ($1\frac{1}{2}''$) from floor. Paint. Make mattress and pillows to fit.

Patio loungers

Mark out strips of ply 4cm ($1\frac{6}{10}''$) wide. From this cut seats, backs, and legs to lengths shown in drawing. Cut two armrests for each lounger. Glue armrests to seat. Fix back in place at an angle. Glue on legs. Paint. Cover seat and back with fabric or self-adhesive vinyl.

Patio table

Cut out top. Cut sides from scraps of 6mm ($\frac{1}{4}''$) ply. Glue sides flush with top. Paint. Cover top with same material used for loungers.

Bathroom

It is not possible to make suitable bathtubs and toilets from wood. Most toyshops sell plastic baths and toilets in a 1:12 scale. A plastic bath could be fitted into a suitable wooden box.

A washbasin can be made as described on page 68, and a bathroom stool as described on page 26.

PATIO LOUNGER

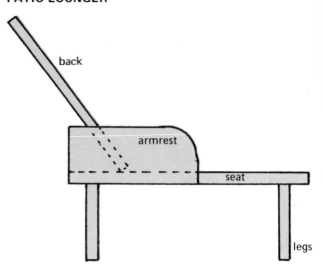

PATIO TABLE

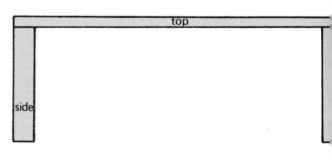

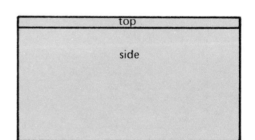

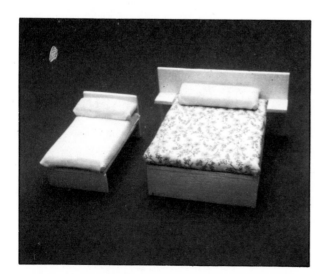

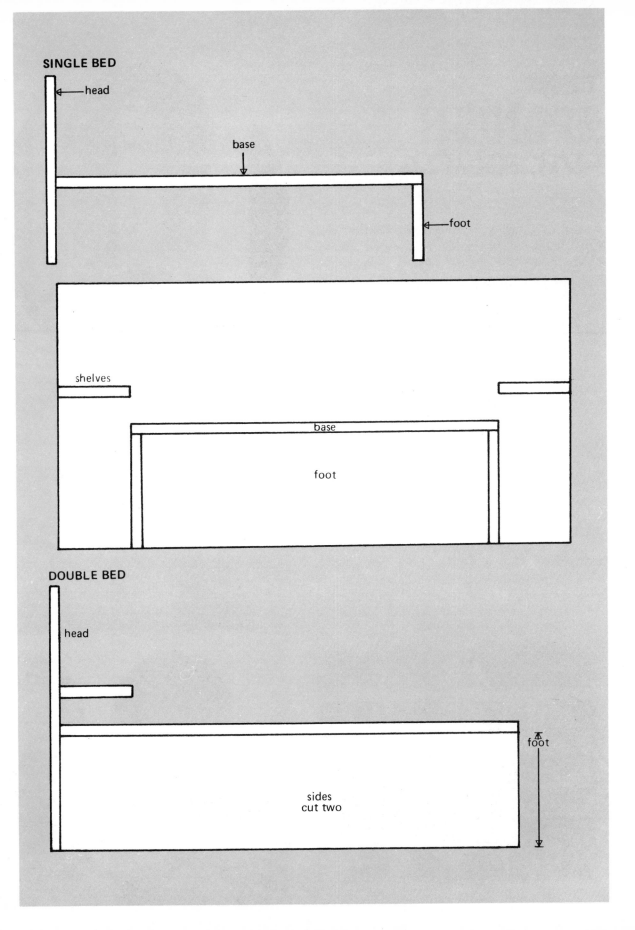

SINGLE BED

head

base

foot

shelves

base

foot

DOUBLE BED

head

foot

sides
cut two

53

THE SPANISH HACIENDA

The arched double doors are made from wood cut out of the door opening in the front wall.

The hacienda is an 'estate or plantation', and the word is of Spanish–American origin. In common parlance, hacienda refers not only to the estate, but particularly to the house on the estate.

The dolls house described here represents some of the more obvious features of the hacienda. The verandah with semicircular arches was designed to provide an outdoor area shielded from the weather. The courtyard garden is surrounded by walls that would have provided protection from intruders as well as privacy. The very long windows, the sloping roofs, and the balcony projecting from the upper part of the house are also typical of many Mediterranean houses.

The furniture within the house is in the Spanish-colonial style, which is, perhaps, difficult to define, but which is typified here by the high ladder-back chairs and the 'carved' bedsteads.

The garden is a special feature of this dolls house. It is not essential to the hacienda, but adds considerably to the play value of the complete house. It is not joined to the house, so it can be moved easily.

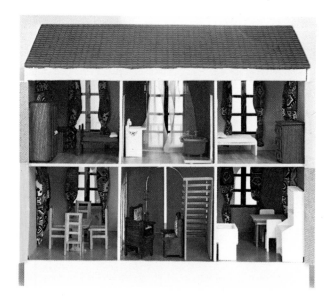

The plywood balcony is glued to the hacienda in front of the hinged french windows.

The balsa wood window frames are glazed with clear acetate.

Plywood strips are glued overlapping the shaped sides to make the verandah steps.

Building the hacienda

Materials

1 sheet 6mm ($\frac{1}{4}$″) plywood 240 × 120cm (8′ × 4′)
1 sheet 3mm ($\frac{1}{8}$″) plywood 240 × 120cm (8′ × 4′)
2m (6′) balsa wood 6 × 1.5mm ($\frac{1}{4}$″ × $\frac{1}{16}$″)
60cm (24″) stripwood 1.2cm ($\frac{1}{2}$″) square
1m (3′) of 6mm ($\frac{1}{4}$″) dowel rod
1.2cm ($\frac{1}{2}$″) panel pins
12 2.5cm (1″) brass hinges with screws to fit
4 hook and eye catches
2 sheets pantile roofing paper for dolls houses
4 polystyrene ceiling tiles 30cm (12″) square
clear acetate sheet
woodworking glue and fabric adhesive
wood stain, varnish, paint, fabric, foam rubber, small
    wooden beads and trimmings
tissue paper, florist's wire, pipecleaners, lichen
modelling clay

The basic structure

Cut out front and two sides. Mark in position of partition walls and tops of floors, shown by broken lines in drawings, on both sides of wood. Cut out window openings and front door. If you are careful in removing the front door, you will be able to use this piece of wood to make the two halves of the front door. Notice that windows on lower half of front are smaller than other windows.

Cut out three floors. They are all the same size, but only the middle floor has slots and stair opening shown in drawing.

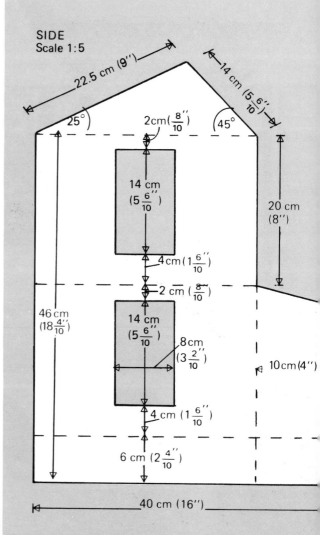

FRONT

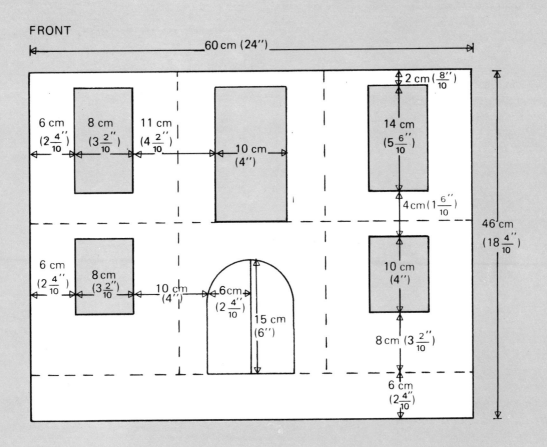

60 cm (24")

6 cm ($2\frac{4}{10}$") 8 cm ($3\frac{2}{10}$") 11 cm ($4\frac{2}{10}$")

10 cm (4")

2 cm ($\frac{8}{10}$")

14 cm ($5\frac{6}{10}$")

4 cm ($1\frac{6}{10}$")

46 cm ($18\frac{4}{10}$")

6 cm ($2\frac{4}{10}$") 8 cm ($3\frac{2}{10}$")

10 cm (4")

6 cm ($2\frac{4}{10}$")

15 cm (6")

10 cm (4")

8 cm ($3\frac{2}{10}$")

6 cm ($2\frac{4}{10}$")

FLOORS (cut 3)

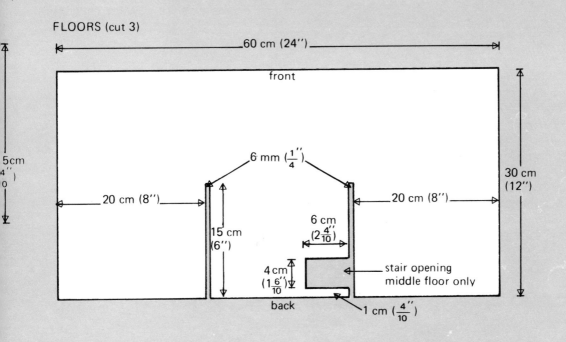

60 cm (24")

front

6 mm ($\frac{1}{4}$")

20 cm (8")

20 cm (8")

30 cm (12")

15 cm (6")

6 cm ($2\frac{4}{10}$")

4 cm ($1\frac{6}{10}$")

stair opening middle floor only

back

1 cm ($\frac{4}{10}$")

5 cm ($\frac{4}{0}$")

57

Cut out two partition walls with slots, arches and doorways. Check that they slot together properly with middle floor. Looking from front of house, arches should be in right-hand partition. Glue partitions and middle floor together, making sure they are square before glue sets. Paint underside of top and middle floors (ceilings)—they are difficult to paint when house is complete. Glue and pin top and lower floors to partitions. Fit on hacienda front and then sides. The sides are wider than the floors so that the front and back fit between them and back wall doors fit flush with them. Glue roof support in middle of top floor.

Cut main roof from 3mm ($\frac{1}{8}$") plywood or hardboard, making pieces long enough to overlap slightly at front and back of house. Glue and pin in place.

Hinge each half of front door in place with two 2.5cm (1") brass hinges, then remove until house has been decorated. Paint doors.

Windows

Make frames from 3mm ($\frac{1}{8}$") thick balsa wood. The frames are drawn full size; trace them onto a piece of greaseproof paper and build over the tracing. In both frames, horizontal strips are glued between vertical bars. Make frames very slightly oversize and trim down to fit tightly in window openings. Paint finished frames. Fix windows in place *after* hacienda has been completely decorated.

Balcony window

Mark out balcony window, shown half size, on 6mm ($\frac{1}{4}$") plywood and cut out with fretsaw. Cut down centre line. After smoothing edges, check fit in window opening. Hinge each half in place with two 2.5cm (1") brass hinges. Remove to decorate and replace after hacienda has been decorated.

For glazing all windows use clear acetate sheeting, which can be purchased from model shops, particularly those specialising in model (balsa) aircraft. Cut acetate to size of frame and fix to back of frame with suitable adhesive. After house has been decorated, fix windows in place with wood glue.

PARTITION WALLS

LEFT WALL

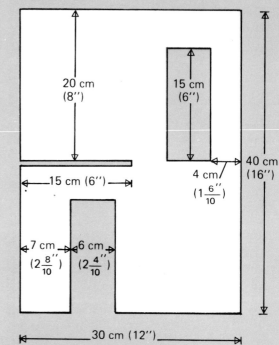

RIGHT WALL

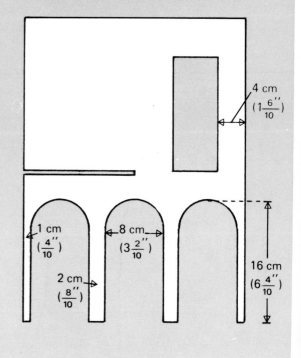

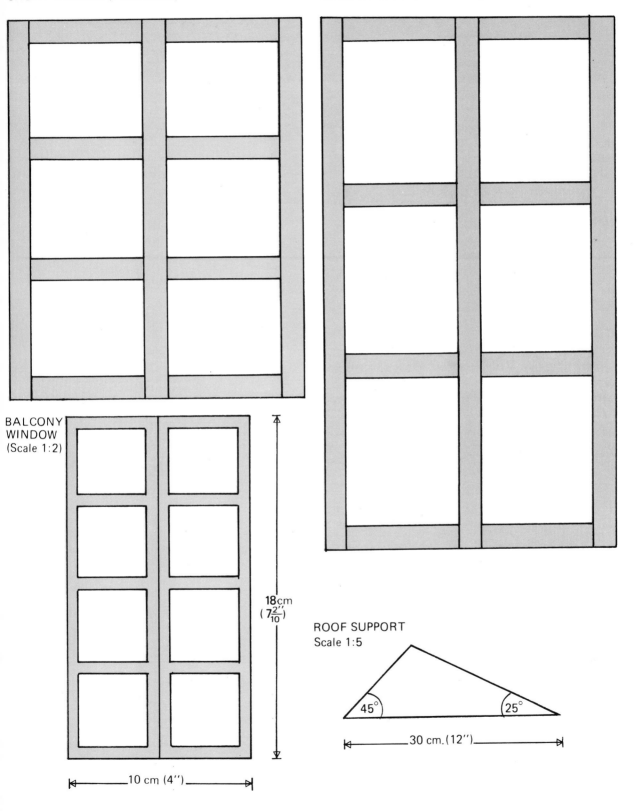

SHORT WINDOW (FULL SIZE)

LONG WINDOW (FULL SIZE)

BALCONY
WINDOW
(Scale 1:2)

18cm
($7\frac{2}{10}''$)

10 cm (4")

ROOF SUPPORT
Scale 1:5

45°   25°

30 cm. (12")

The verandah

Cut out verandah arches, floor and supporting wall. Fix 60cm (24″) length of 1.2cm ($\frac{1}{2}$″) square stripwood to front wall of hacienda so that top of strip is 5.4cm ($2\frac{1}{10}$″) from base. Pin and glue arches to floor, then fix floor to supporting wall. Check that verandah fits onto front of hacienda between the two side extensions, which form verandah walls.

Decorate verandah and front and sides of hacienda. Stain verandah floor and supporting wall with wood stain, then cover with two coats of polyurethane varnish. Paint verandah arches and front and side walls of hacienda with white vinyl emulsion paint. After paint is dry, fix verandah to hacienda and make its roof from hardboard or 3mm ($\frac{1}{8}$″) ply. The roof should overlap arches by same amount as main roof overlaps front and back. To finish roofs cover them with green pantile paper, which is specially made for dolls houses. If you prefer, paint roofs with green emulsion paint; do not use gloss—it spoils the appearance of the hacienda.

The balcony

Cut out balcony floor and top rail. Clamp pieces together. Using hand drill with drill bit that will make a hole into which 6mm ($\frac{1}{4}$″) dowel rod will fit tightly, drill holes through both pieces as shown on drawing. Cut eleven 6cm ($2\frac{4}{10}$″) lengths of dowel rod and glue into holes in floor and rail. Paint balcony white. When dry, glue in position on front of hacienda.

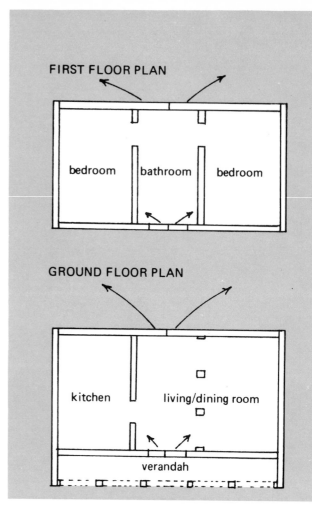

FIRST FLOOR PLAN

bedroom   bathroom   bedroom

GROUND FLOOR PLAN

kitchen   living/dining room

verandah

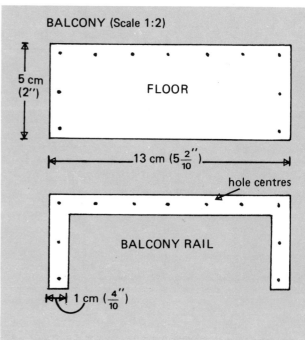

BALCONY (Scale 1:2)

5 cm (2″)

FLOOR

13 cm ($5\frac{2}{10}$″)

hole centres

BALCONY RAIL

1 cm ($\frac{4}{10}$″)

VERANDAH: VERANDAH ARCHES (Scale 1:5)

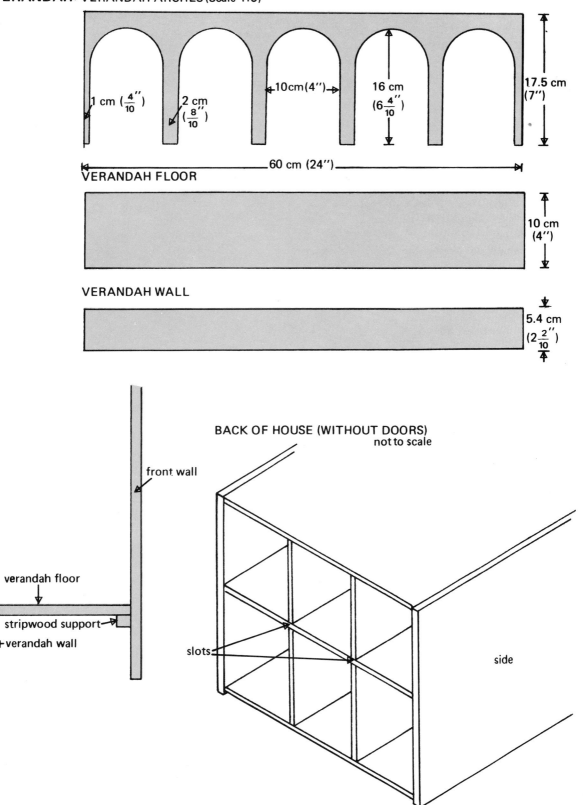

1 cm ($\frac{4''}{10}$)

2 cm ($\frac{8''}{10}$)

←10cm(4")→

16 cm ($6\frac{4''}{10}$)

17.5 cm (7")

←——————— 60 cm (24") ———————→

VERANDAH FLOOR

10 cm (4")

VERANDAH WALL

5.4 cm ($2\frac{2''}{10}$)

es

front wall

verandah floor

stripwood support

verandah wall

BACK OF HOUSE (WITHOUT DOORS)
not to scale

slots

side

The back

The back is same size as front, but is cut into four pieces, as shown. Fit top piece across back of hacienda just under roof. Fit bottom piece flush across back in line with bottom floor. Using six 2.5cm (1″) brass hinges, hinge remaining two pieces to sides to form back doors. Use small hook and eye catches to hold doors shut.

Staircase

Cut rectangle 18×19.5cm ($7\frac{2}{10}″ \times 7\frac{8}{10}″$) from 3mm ($\frac{1}{8}″$) plywood. Mark out as shown in drawing opposite. Cut along zig-zag line to make two identical pieces. These form the two sides of staircase. Cut out twelve steps. Glue left end of steps onto risers on one staircase side, fitting flush with side. When glue has set, glue steps onto right side overlapping side 1cm ($\frac{4}{10}″$). After painting or varnishing, place staircase under stair opening in middle floor.

Verandah steps

Cut two sides and two steps from 3mm ($\frac{1}{8}″$) plywood. Glue steps to sides so that they overlap sides 1cm ($\frac{4}{10}″$) on each side. Stain same colour as verandah floor and supporting wall.

Decorating the interior

The ceilings should already be painted. Paint or paper all interior walls. If walls are being papered, follow instructions given in **Before you begin . . .** (page 9).

Stain floors of hacienda with light-coloured wood stain and two coats of polyurethane varnish, or cover with self-adhesive vinyl paper.

Curtains

Cut suitable fabric into pieces 9×19cm ($3\frac{6}{10}″ \times 7\frac{6}{10}″$). Smear fabric adhesive along top and bottom of each curtain, then bunch fabric together. Tie tightly about one-third of way up from bottom. After windows have been glued in place, glue curtains to either side of them so that they can be seen from outside, but do not obscure view of inside. Glue braid or similar trimming over top of window for neat finish.

STAIRCASE
(Scale 1:2)

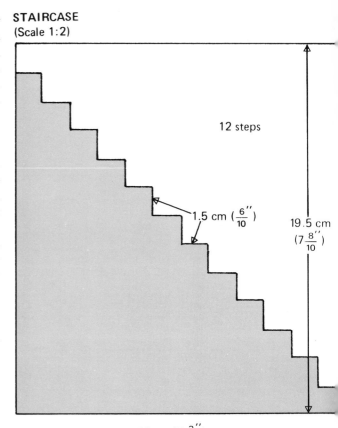

12 steps

1.5 cm ($\frac{6}{10}″$)

19.5 cm ($7\frac{8}{10}″$)

18 cm ($7\frac{2}{10}″$)

step

overhang

(not to scale)

left   right

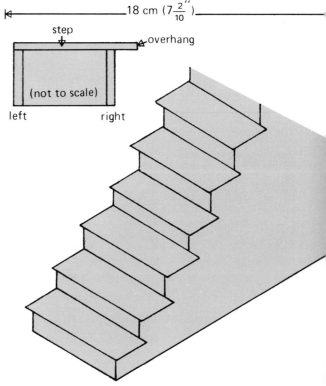

62

BACK

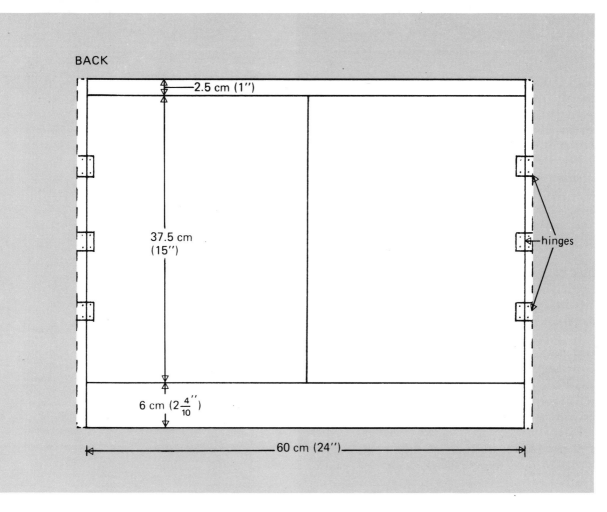

2.5 cm (1")

37.5 cm (15")

hinges

6 cm (2 4/10")

60 cm (24")

VERANDAH STEPS

SIDE STEP

STEP (FULL SIZE)

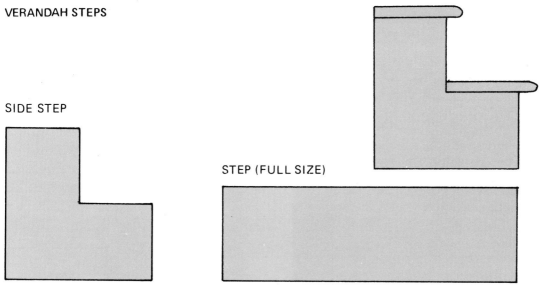

Furniture

All furniture is made from 3mm ($\frac{1}{8}''$) plywood and patterns are given full size unless stated otherwise. Trace patterns onto thin card and use them as templates. If different or additional pieces are wanted, remember that all the houses in this book are designed to a 1:12 scale so that the furniture is interchangeable. Paint, varnish or stain all furniture.

Living room settee and armchairs

Cut sides for settee and armchairs from same pattern. Cut seats for armchairs 3.5 × 4cm ($1\frac{4}{10}'' \times 1\frac{6}{10}''$) and seat for settee 3.5 × 8cm ($1\frac{4}{10}'' \times 3\frac{2}{10}''$). Cut armchair backs 5.5 × 4cm ($2\frac{2}{10}'' \times 1\frac{6}{10}''$), and settee back 5.5 × 8cm ($2\frac{2}{10}'' \times 3\frac{2}{10}''$). Glue matching back and seat to one side as shown by broken lines in drawing. When glue is dry, add other side.

Upholstery

To upholster seats and backs of armchairs and settee cut pieces of thin card to size. Use these as templates to cut pieces of foam rubber 1cm ($\frac{4}{10}''$) thick. Cut pieces of fabric 1.5cm ($\frac{1}{2}''$) wider all round than template. Place fabric face down on work surface and put foam rubber and then card in middle of it. Put fabric adhesive on card and pull fabric onto it. Be careful with the corners—you may need to trim off some fabric. When glue is dry, glue cushions to backs and seats. All upholstery, mattresses and pillows are made this way.

Dining table

Cut out two legs, strip, and top 8 × 6cm ($3\frac{2}{10}'' \times 2\frac{4}{10}''$). Fix strip into slots in legs, then glue legs to top.

Dining chairs

Make four. For each one cut out two sides, back, and seat 3.5 × 3cm ($1\frac{4}{10}'' \times 1\frac{2}{10}''$). Glue back and seat to one side. When glue is dry, add other side.

Sideboard

This is a simple box construction. Cut out front, back, two sides. Glue sides to front and back. Measure top, cut out wood and glue in place. Round off front edge of top with fine sandpaper.

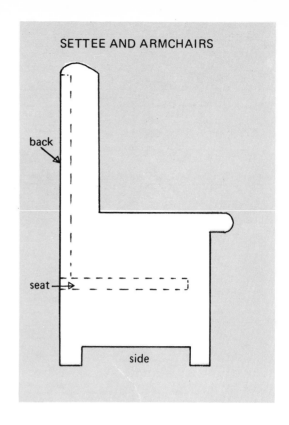

SETTEE AND ARMCHAIRS

back

seat

side

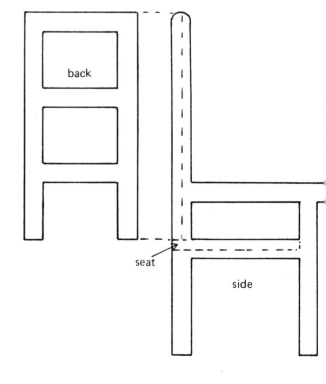

DINING CHAIRS

back

seat

side

SIDEBOARD

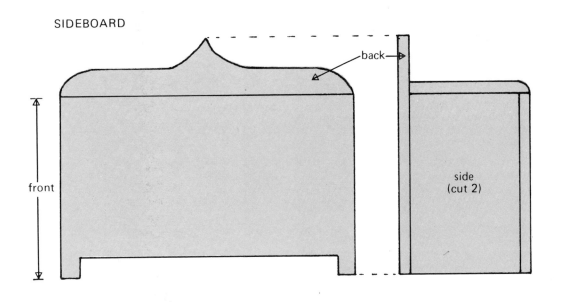

DINING TABLE

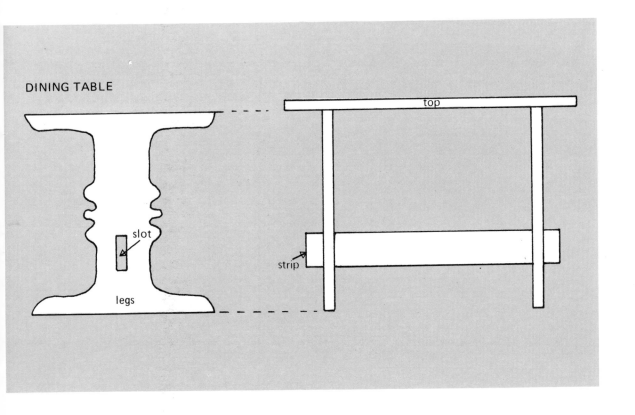

Beds

A single and a double bed are shown. Cut out head and foot of each bed. Cut single bed base 9 × 6.5cm ($3\frac{6}{10}''$ × $2\frac{6}{10}''$), and double bed base 10 × 8cm ($4''$ × $3\frac{2}{10}''$). Glue base to head and foot. Make mattresses and pillows in the same way as described for upholstering.

Chest of drawers

The chest of drawers is a simple box construction. Cut out two sides, front, back, and top. Glue sides to front and back, then glue on top. Cut out three drawer fronts and glue on front. Cut wooden beads in half with sharp craft knife to make drawer handles.

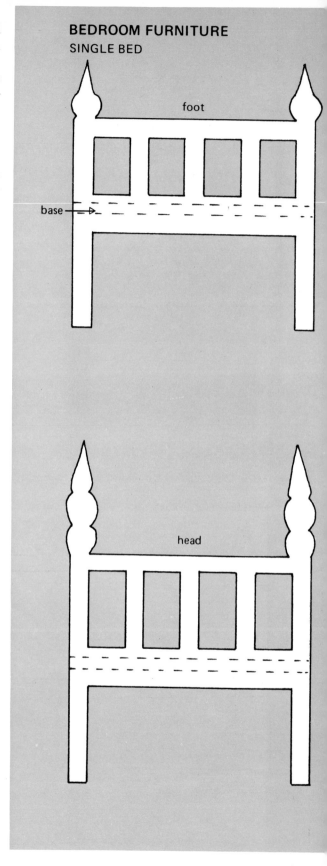

BEDROOM FURNITURE
SINGLE BED

foot

base

head

DOUBLE BED

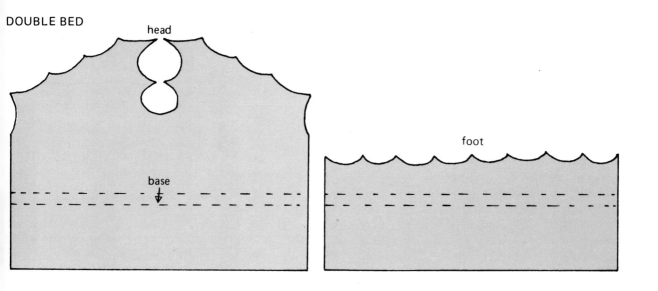

head

base

foot

CHEST OF DRAWERS

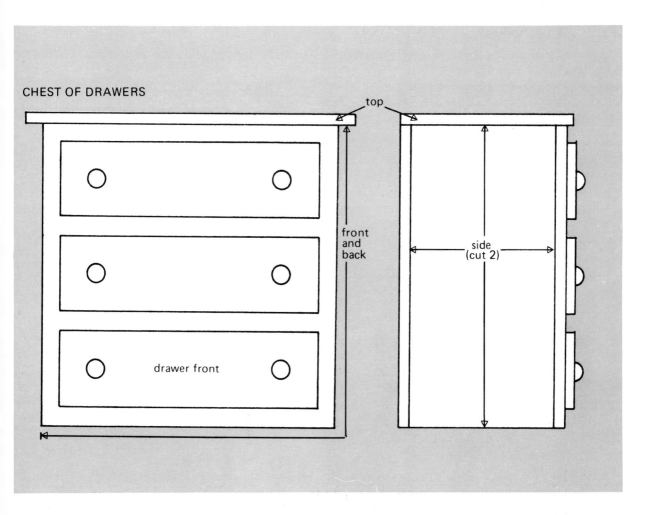

top

front
and
back

side
(cut 2)

drawer front

Dressing table

Cut out back with mirrors as one piece. Cut out circles for mirrors and cover back with kitchen foil and a piece of thin card. Cut out front, two sides 5×4cm ($2'' \times 1\frac{6}{10}''$), and top 9×5cm ($3\frac{6}{10}'' \times 2''$). Glue sides to back and front. Glue on top. Cut three drawer fronts and glue to front. Split wooden beads in half with sharp craft knife and glue to front for drawer handles.

Washbasin

The washbasin is built around a small plastic dish such as butter might be packed in for restaurants or cafeterias. Cut back, two sides, and top 6×4.5cm ($2\frac{4}{10}'' \times 1\frac{8}{10}''$). Glue sides to back, then cut out shelf to fit between sides and glue in place. Cut out rectangle in top along solid line. Glue rim of plastic dish, shown by broken line, to top, then glue top in place. Cut two tap (faucet) shapes and glue to top.

If you cannot find a small plastic container, make a shallow wooden box and glue in place.

Wardrobe

The wardrobe is a simple box construction. Cut out front, back, two sides, and top and bottom. Glue top and bottom to sides, then glue to front and back. Cut out door fronts and glue to front. Make handles from wooden bead halves. Cut plinth and glue under wardrobe bottom.

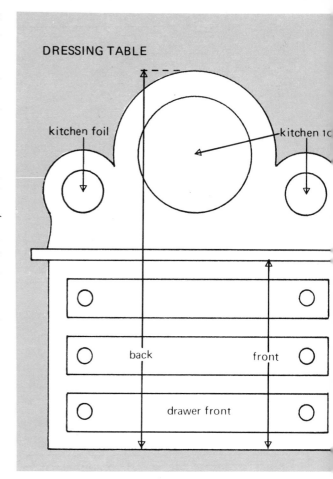

DRESSING TABLE

kitchen foil kitchen 1c

back front

drawer front

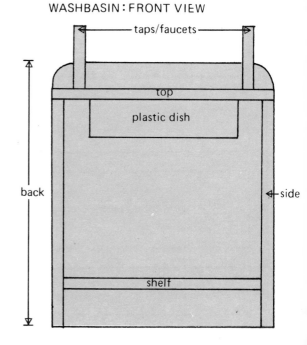

WASHBASIN: FRONT VIEW

taps/faucets

top

plastic dish

back

side

shelf

WARDROBE

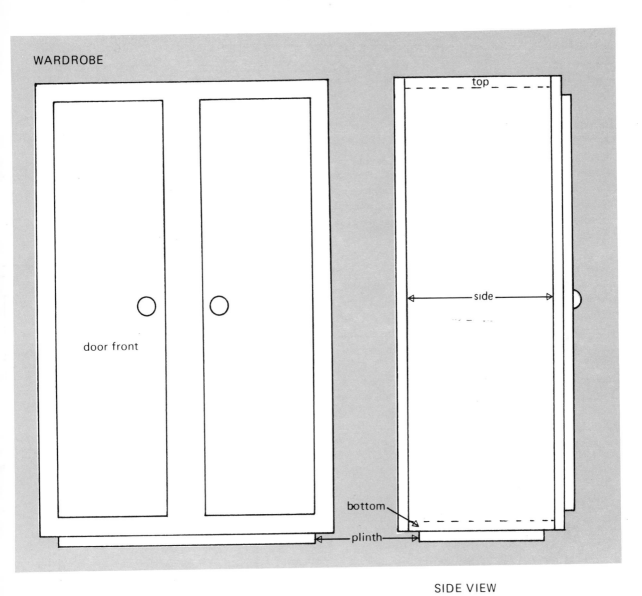

door front

top

side

bottom

plinth

TOP VIEW

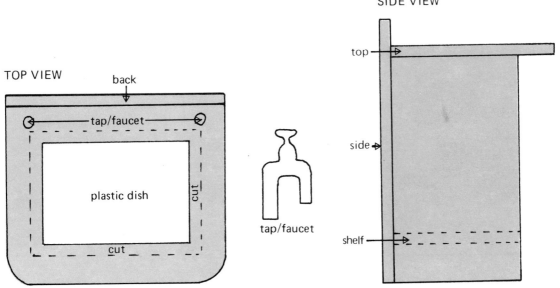

back

tap/faucet

cut

cut

plastic dish

tap/faucet

SIDE VIEW

top

side

shelf

Kitchen chair

Cut out back and back legs as one piece. Cut out area between broken lines for front legs, and seat 3.5×2.5cm ($1\frac{4}{10}'' \times 1''$). Glue seat to front legs, then to back, checking that structure is square before glue sets.

Kitchen table

Cut out top 6×8cm ($2\frac{4}{10}'' \times 3\frac{2}{10}''$), six strips 6×1cm ($2\frac{4}{10}'' \times \frac{4}{10}''$), and two strips 4×1cm ($1\frac{6}{10}'' \times \frac{4}{10}''$). Glue two long and two short strips together end to end to make frame. Glue frame under table top, leaving equal space all round. Use remaining four strips for legs. Glue to table top inside corners of frame.

Kitchen sink

Cut out two sides, back and front. Glue together. Measure space between legs for bottom. Cut out and glue in place. Cut out top, cutting out inner rectangle along solid line. Glue frame to top of sink. You could add taps (faucets) as for washbasin.

Kitchen shelf unit

Cut out back, two sides, two shelves 2.5×6.9cm ($1'' \times 2\frac{8}{10}''$), and two shelves 4.5×6.9cm ($1\frac{8}{10}'' \times 2\frac{8}{10}''$). Glue shelves between sides, then glue unit to back.

SMALL KITCHEN CHAIR

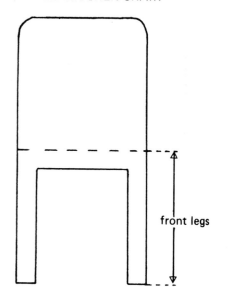

front legs

KITCHEN TABLE

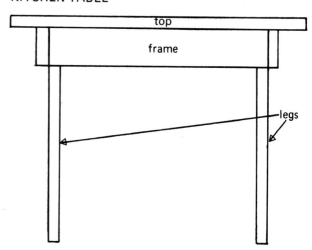

top

frame

legs

KITCHEN SINK

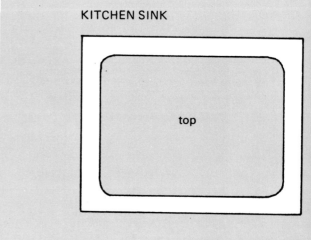

top

KITCHEN SHELF UNIT

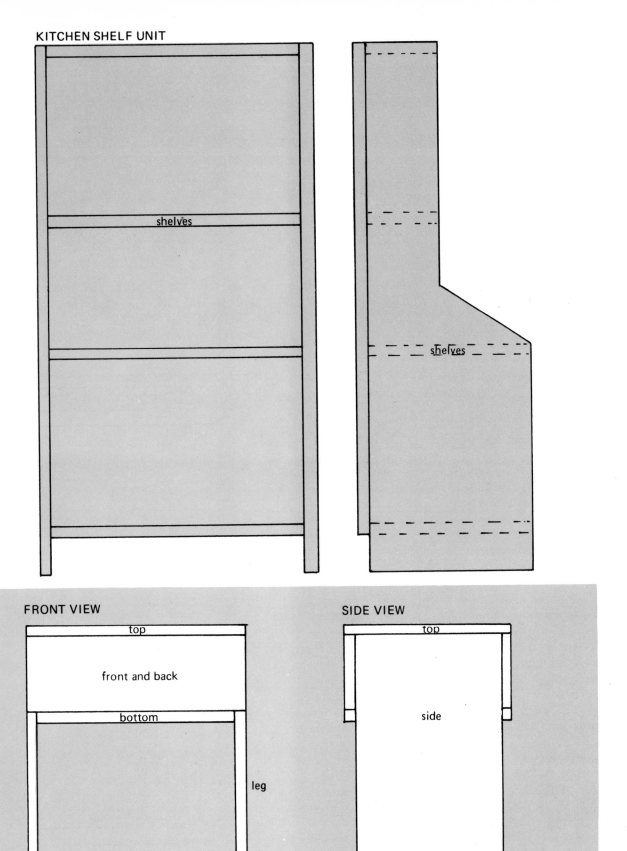

shelves

shelves

FRONT VIEW

top

front and back

bottom

leg

SIDE VIEW

top

side

The garden

Make base of garden from piece of 3mm ($\frac{1}{8}''$) plywood 61.2cm ($24\frac{1}{2}''$) wide—as wide as the hacienda —and 40cm (16″) deep. Using 6mm ($\frac{1}{4}''$) plywood, make walls 13cm ($5\frac{2}{10}''$) high to lengths indicated on diagram.

Mark out path as shown and glue coarse sandpaper over marked area. Make small bricks from modelling clay to line path as shown. When clay is dry, glue bricks over edge of sandpaper. Make another flower-bed in centre of path with circle of bricks.

Trees and bushes

Take six to eight pipecleaners and start twisting them together tightly from one end to form tree trunk. About two-thirds of the way up trunk bend out one pipecleaner to form branch. Do this with others at irregular intervals. Bend branches to pleasing shapes. Untwist cleaners a little way at base of trunk. Surround base with modelling clay, forming cone shape with flat bottom. Paint tree with mixture of emulsion paint, cellulose wood filler, and poster colour. The wood filler stiffens the tree so that it holds its shape firmly, but can still be bent to different shapes. For foliage buy 'lichen' and glue to tree branches. Lichen is a synthetic material usually sold in shops that specialise in materials for railway modellers, who use it to make scenery around their models.

Flowers

Make flowers from coloured tissue paper and green florist's wire. Cut a suitable length of wire. Glue a small piece of tissue paper to one end of wire, twisting it round to form small knob. Now cut some tissue paper into 8cm ($3\frac{2}{10}''$) squares. Fold squares several times to make 2cm ($\frac{8}{10}''$) squares. Keeping thickest single fold at bottom, draw petal patterns shown opposite onto squares. Cut out petals with sharp scissors and unfold. Push uncovered end of wire through centre of one layer of petals. Push petals up to small knob and glue in place on stem. Add six to eight more layers of petals, gluing each in place. Cut leaves from green tissue paper and glue onto stems. Push stems into small cones of modelling clay. When clay is dry, paint it and flower beds suitable shade of brown.

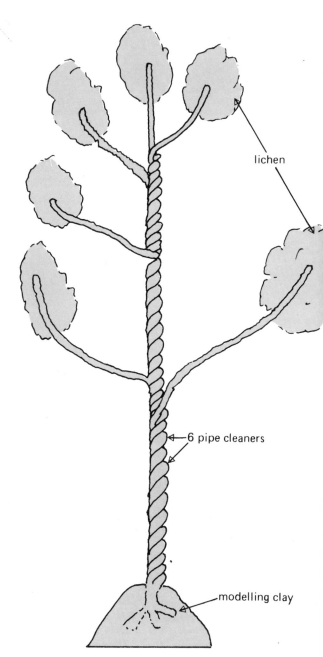

lichen

6 pipe cleaners

modelling clay

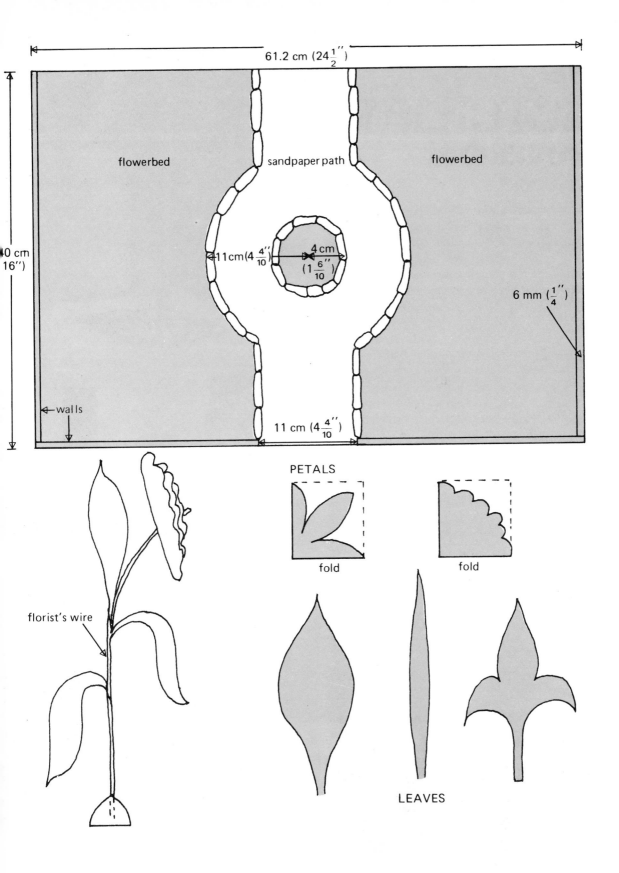

61.2 cm (24½")

flowerbed   sandpaper path   flowerbed

40 cm
(16")

11cm(4 4/10")   4 cm
                      (1 6/10")

6 mm (¼")

walls

11 cm (4 4/10")

florist's wire

PETALS

fold   fold

LEAVES

THE VICTORIAN MANSION

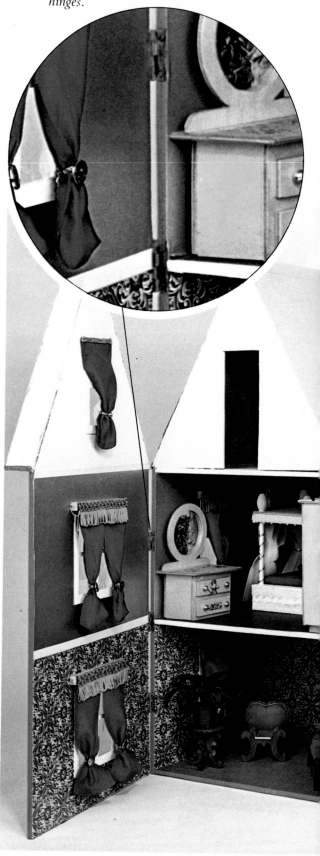

During the nineteenth century England was enjoying a period of industrial supremacy brought about by the Industrial Revolution, which had begun in the eighteenth century and probably reached its climax about 1850. The population was divided into three distinct classes: the very rich upper class, the middle income middle class, and the poor working class.

There is a saying that an Englishman's home is his castle, and the middle classes in Victorian England certainly did build a number of mock castles. More often, however, they built themselves large, solid, and frequently uncomfortable mansions. These were usually of red brick with patterns of yellow brick to relieve the plainness of the walls. The roofs were made of blue-grey Welsh slate. The Victorian mansion was a means whereby the successful industrialist or merchant could display his success to the world.

Inside the house the furniture was heavy and ornate. By modern standards the rooms were too crowded, but this abundant display of possessions was typical of the Victorian era.

This dolls house, the largest in the book, includes some of the typical features of a Victorian mansion.

The chimneys are simple box constructions with pieces of dowelling for chimneypots.

The windows have double cardboard frames and clear acetate glazing.

Building
the mansion

Materials

1 sheet 6mm ($\frac{1}{4}''$) ply 240 × 120cm (8' × 4')
1 sheet 6mm ($\frac{1}{4}''$) ply 120 × 120cm (4' × 4')
1 sheet 3mm ($\frac{1}{8}''$) ply 240 × 120cm (8' × 4')
16cm of 1.2cm ($\frac{1}{2}''$) dowel rod
4 sheets thin white card 64 × 52cm (26" × 21")
1 sheet thin black card 64 × 52cm (26" × 21")
16 2.5cm (1") brass hinges with screws to fit
1.2cm ($\frac{1}{2}''$) panel pins
clear acetate sheet
self-adhesive vinyl
woodworking glue and fabric adhesive
2m (6') fringe
paint, woodstain, varnish, foam rubber, fabric, beads
trimming

The basic structure

The whole house, except the roof, is made from 6mm
($\frac{1}{4}''$) plywood.

Mark out the front and back to dimensions shown.
The pitch of roof is 60°. Mark in position of
dividing walls and tops of floors, as shown by broken
lines, on both sides of wood. Cut out window and
door openings with a fretsaw. Keep front and back
door pieces to use as doors. Cut down solid line
marked 'cut' in diagram. The two parts of front and
the two parts of back will be hinged to sides so that
interior can be reached.

Cut out five partition walls.

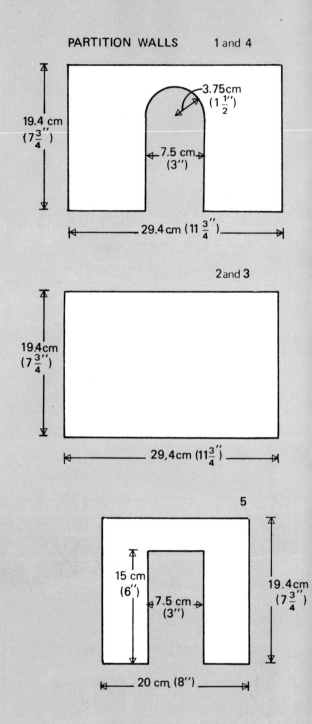

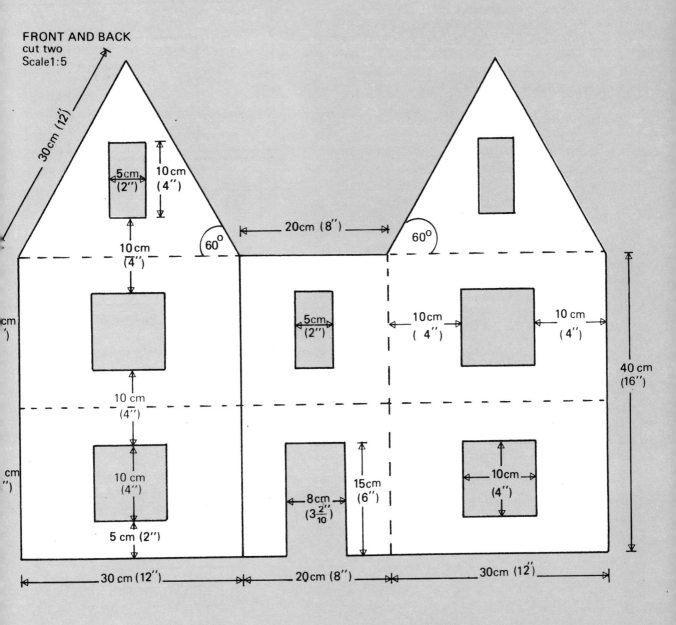

FRONT AND BACK
cut two
Scale 1:5

30cm (12")

5 cm (2")

10 cm (4")

10 cm (4")

60°

20cm (8")

60°

5cm (2")

10cm (4")

10 cm (4")

10 cm (4")

40 cm (16")

10 cm (4")

10 cm (4")

15cm (6")

8cm (3 2/10")

10cm (4")

5 cm (2")

30 cm (12")

20cm (8")

30cm (12")

cm ')

cm ")

77

Cut out the two sides. Each side has four single windows. Mark in position of top of middle floor.

Make three floors. They are all the same size. The ground floor and top floor are plain, but the middle floor has an opening for stairs and two slots, cut as shown, into which dividing walls fit.

Cut two dividing walls. They have door openings from hall or landing into various rooms. (The right wall referred to on drawing is right wall when looking from front of house.)

Check that dividing walls fit squarely with middle floor, ground floor and top floor. Paint ceilings of middle and top floors with two coats of white emulsion paint. The painting is an easy job now, but much more difficult when the house is assembled.

Check that partition walls are a good fit. Glue and pin together middle floor, dividing walls, and five partition walls. When glue is dry, pin and glue sides to ground floor. Fit in interior walls and floor unit. Lastly, pin and glue top floor in position.

Using three hinges for each piece, hinge two parts of back and two parts of front to sides. To make parts fit well, hinges should be rebated.

Cut eight double and fourteen single size lintels and windowsills from 6mm ($\frac{1}{4}$″) plywood. Paint white or other suitable colour.

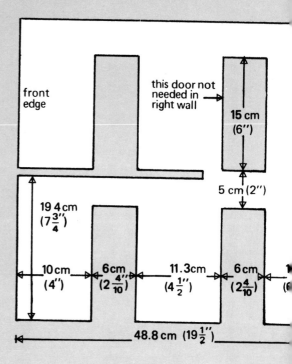

DIVIDING WALLS (cut 2) Scale 1:5

front edge

this door not needed in right wall →

15 cm (6″)

5 cm (2″)

19 4 cm ($7\frac{3}{4}$″)

10 cm (4″)

6 cm ($2\frac{4}{10}$)

11.3cm ($4\frac{1}{2}$″)

6 cm ($2\frac{4}{10}$)

48.8 cm ($19\frac{1}{2}$″)

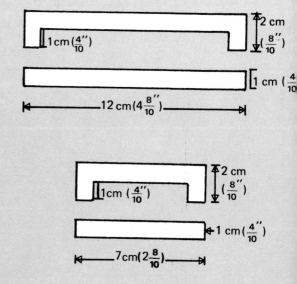

LINTELS AND SILLS Scale 1:2

1 cm ($\frac{4}{10}$″)

2 cm ($\frac{8}{10}$″)

1 cm ($\frac{4}{10}$)

12 cm ($4\frac{8}{10}$″)

1cm ($\frac{4}{10}$″)

2 cm ($\frac{8}{10}$″)

1 cm ($\frac{4}{10}$″)

7cm ($2\frac{8}{10}$″)

SIDES (cut 2) Scale 1:5

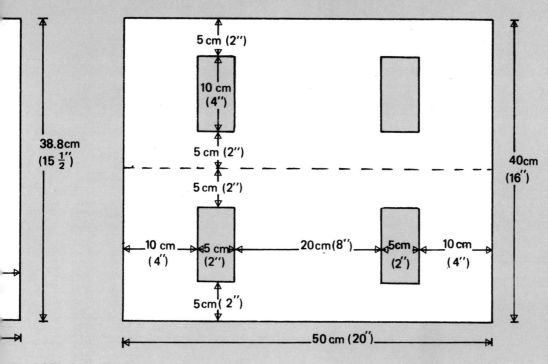

5 cm (2″)

10 cm (4″)

5 cm (2″)

38.8cm (15 ½″)

5 cm (2″)

40cm (16″)

10 cm (4″)   5 cm (2″)   20cm(8″)   5cm (2″)   10 cm (4″)

5cm(2″)

50 cm (20″)

FLOORS Scale 1:5

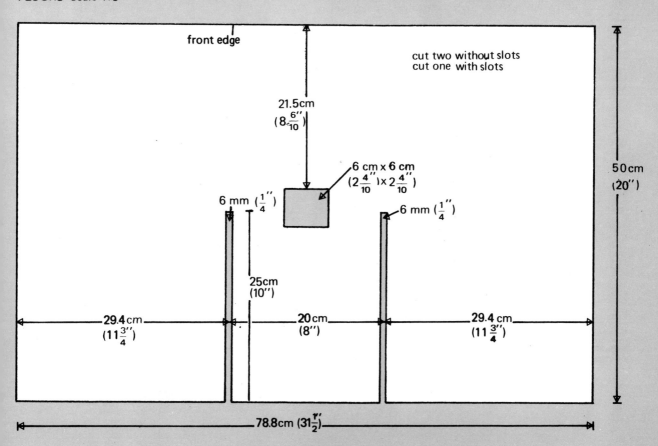

front edge

cut two without slots
cut one with slots

21.5cm (8 6/10″)

6 cm x 6 cm (2 4/10″ x 2 4/10″)

6 mm (¼″)   6 mm (¼″)

25cm (10″)

29.4 cm (11 ¾″)   20 cm (8″)   29.4 cm (11 ¾″)

50cm (20″)

78.8cm (31 ½″)

Roof

Cut out four roof supports. Pin and glue in place, matching them up with gables on front and back of house.

Cut five roof pieces from 3mm ($\frac{1}{8}$") plywood or hardboard. The roof fits flush with back and front of open house, and overlaps sides to make eaves about 6mm ($\frac{1}{4}$") deep. The middle part of roof between two pitched roofs is flat. Make eaves over four gables from strips of wood 2.5cm (1") wide. Pin and glue them to front and back of house—up each side of gables and across flat roof in middle, as shown in colour photograph on pages 74–75.

Cover roof with strips of thin card cut as shown opposite. Start gluing strips at eaves, overlapping them so that glued edges are covered and slates alternate. Close front and back of house while doing this so that eaves are covered too. When glue is dry, use a sharp knife to cut through slates so that front and back can open again.

Finishing touches

Paint roof with two or three coats of blue-grey emulsion paint.

Paint exterior of house with brick red emulsion paint. You could, if you prefer, cover walls with brick patterned paper specially made for dolls houses, but paint is harder wearing and easily cleaned.

Glue lintels and windowsills in place.

Cut eight pieces of card 2cm ($\frac{3}{4}$") wide and 30.5cm (12") long for barge boards. Paint white and glue to eaves of gables at front and back of house.

Fit front and back doors in place with 2.5cm (1") brass hinges. Remove doors and paint them. To make front door more impressive, glue on card panels before painting. Paint both doors with black gloss paint.

Make two chimney stacks. Cut out four pieces of wood for each, and pin and glue together as shown opposite. Paint stacks red and cover open tops with black card. Cut four 4cm (1$\frac{1}{2}$") lengths of 1.2cm ($\frac{1}{2}$") dowel for chimneys. Paint dowels black and glue on top of chimney stack.

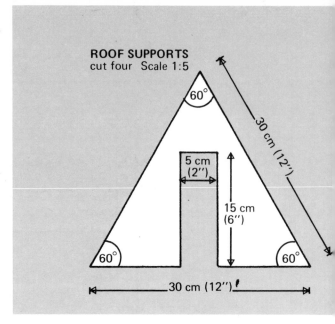

ROOF SUPPORTS
cut four Scale 1:5

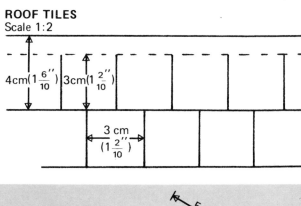

ROOF TILES
Scale 1:2

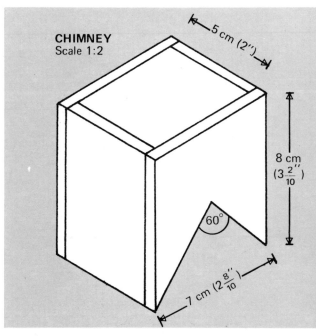

CHIMNEY
Scale 1:2

GROUND FLOOR

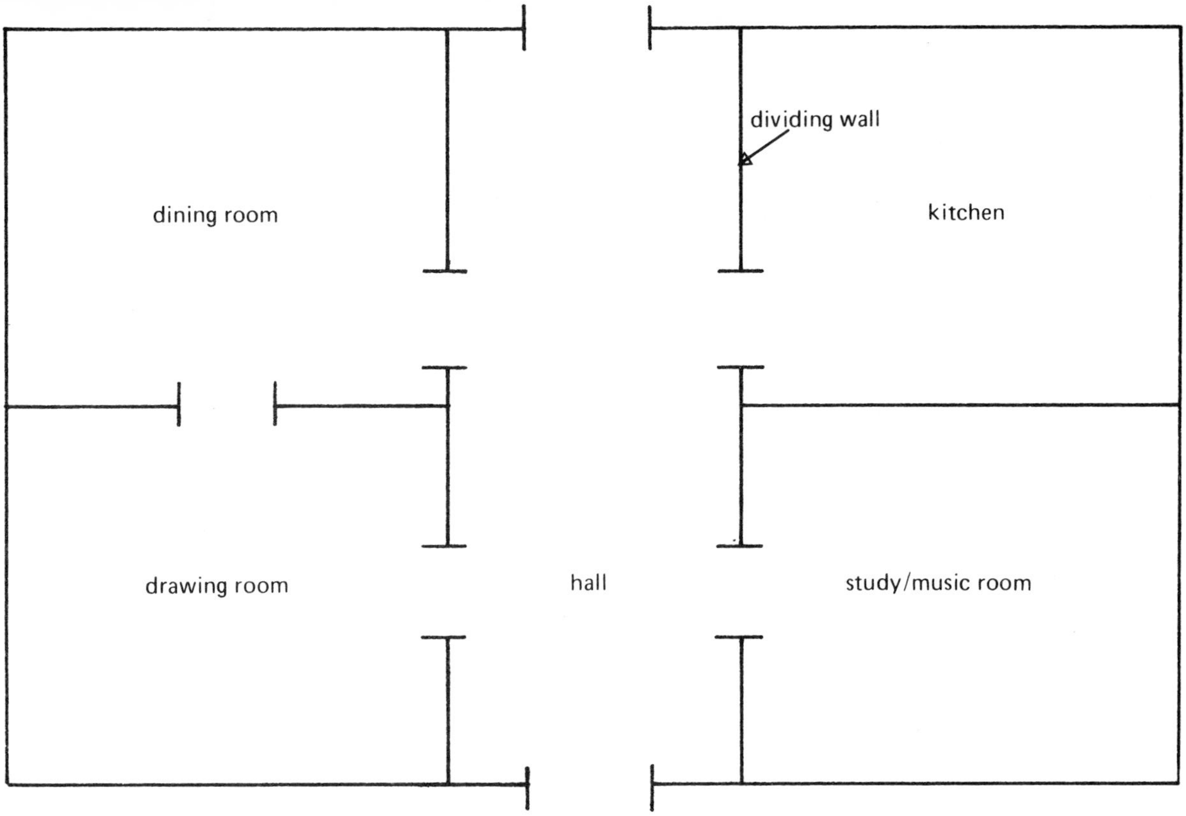

dining room

dividing wall

kitchen

drawing room

hall

study/music room

FIRST FLOOR

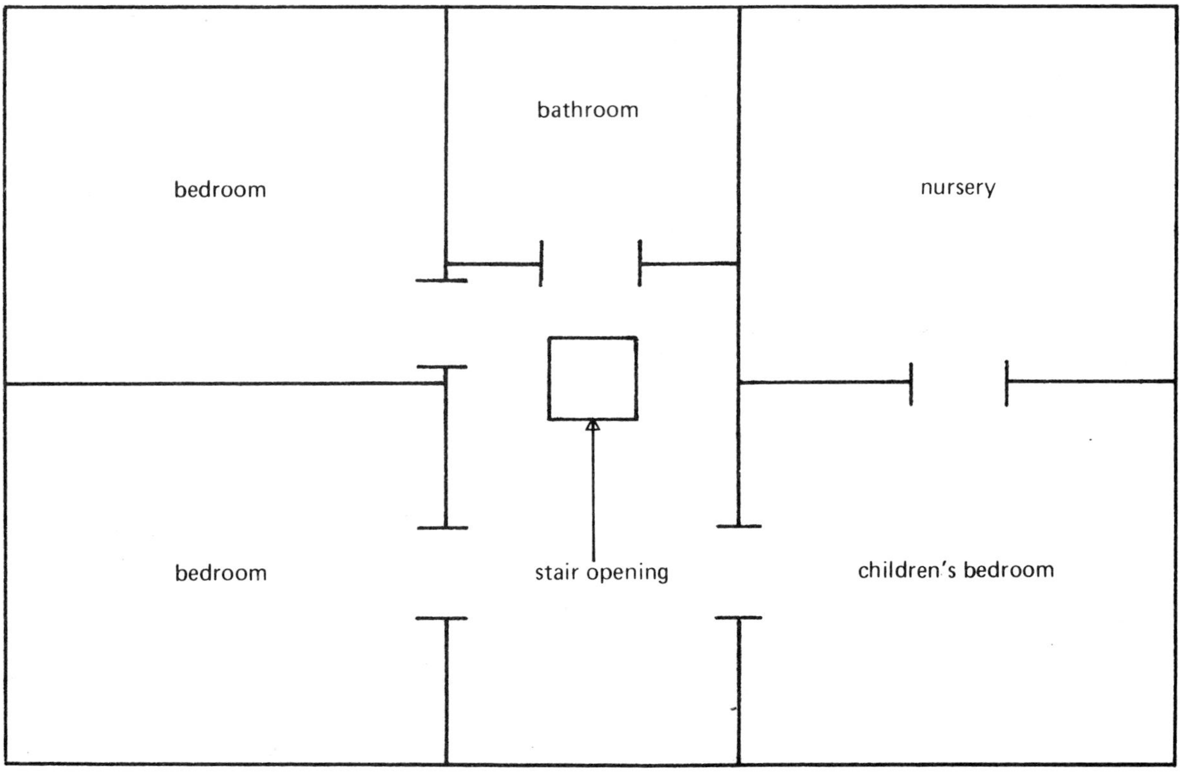

bedroom

bathroom

nursery

bedroom

stair opening

children's bedroom

Window frames

Each window frame is made from an inner frame (solid line) and an outer frame (broken line). You will need inner and outer frames for eight double and fourteen single windows.

Draw frames on thick card and cut out with sharp craft knife. Cover with two coats of white emulsion paint. Trim outer (smaller) frames to fit tightly in window openings. Number frames and openings so that trimmed frames can later be fitted into correct window openings.

Cut clear acetate sheet to size shown by dotted line. Glue acetate between inner and outer frames. *After* rooms have been papered (see Decorating), glue frames inside rooms around window openings with outer frames fitting into openings.

Staircase

The staircase is made from thick card. It could also be made from wood by adapting instructions for staircase in Chalet.

Draw out nine stairs with gluing tabs—the pattern given is full size for first few stairs. Score solid lines, including bases of gluing tabs, on front of card; score broken lines on back of card. Fold card to form nine stairs.

Cut out banisters and sides of staircase. Glue stairs between two sides. Cut card to fit back of staircase and glue in place. Trim staircase, if necessary, so that it is a tight fit between hall floor and stair opening in middle floor. Give staircase two coats of emulsion paint and fit in place.

Decorating the interior

For walls use wallpaper specially made for dolls houses, and follow directions given in **Before you begin . . .** (page 9).

Using a sharp craft knife, cut out 3cm ($1\frac{2}{10}$″) squares accurately from thin card. Cut some black, some white; paint some yellow and some red. Tile hall floor with black and white squares, and kitchen floor with red and yellow squares. Cover other floors with self-adhesive vinyl sheeting.

STAIRS
Full size

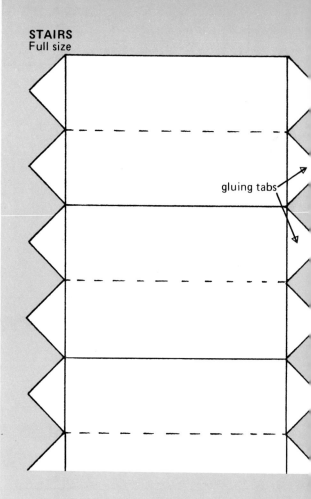

gluing tabs

HOW TO FOLD STAIRS

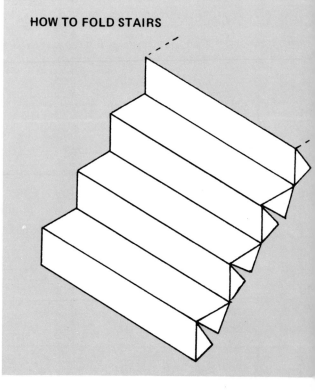

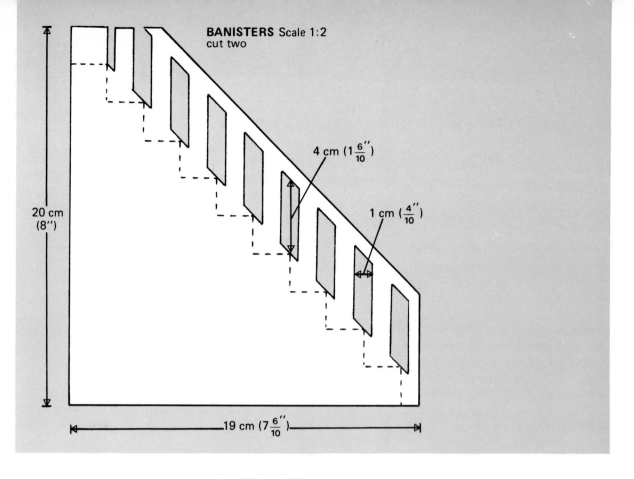

BANISTERS Scale 1:2
cut two

20 cm (8'')

4 cm ($1\frac{6}{10}$'')

1 cm ($\frac{4}{10}$'')

19 cm ($7\frac{6}{10}$'')

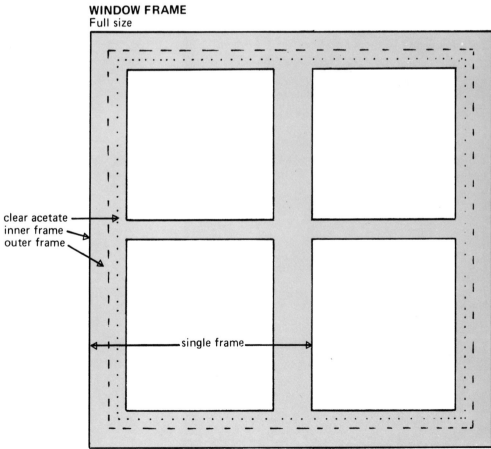

WINDOW FRAME
Full size

clear acetate
inner frame
outer frame

single frame

Curtains

Using fairly thin fabric, cut pieces 15 × 17cm (6″ × 6¾″) for double windows, and 10 × 17cm (4″ × 6¾″) for single windows. Using fabric adhesive, make 1cm (½″) hems down the two long sides and across the bottom. For double window curtains glue top raw edge to 13cm (5″) lengths of 1.2cm (½″) square wood, which form pelmets, and cut curtains in half lengthways. For single window curtains, glue top raw edge to 8cm (3″) lengths of 1.2cm (½″) square wood to form pelmets. Do not cut single curtains and do not make pelmets for the four single windows in the gables, as they would prevent the front and back parts closing. Complete pelmets by gluing on lengths of fringe. Use ribbon or gift-wrap twine to tie all curtains tightly about one-third of the way up.

Furniture

All the furniture is made from 3mm (⅛″) plywood and patterns are given full size unless stated otherwise. Trace patterns onto thin card and use them as templates.

Dining room chairs

Cut out the back, front and seat. Smooth rough edges with glasspaper. Glue seat to back. Then glue front legs to front seat edge. Check that chair is square before glue has set. Paint or varnish chair.

Upholstery

To upholster the chair, cut a piece of thin card the size of the seat. Use this as a template to cut a piece of foam rubber 1cm ($\frac{4}{10}$″) thick. Cut a piece of fabric 1.5cm (½″) wider all round than seat. Place fabric face down on work surface and put foam rubber and then card in middle of it. Put fabric adhesive on card and pull fabric onto it. Be careful with the corners—you may need to trim off some fabric. When glue is dry, glue cushion to seat. All unholstery, mattresses and bed pillows are made in the same way.

Table

Cut out table top and two sets of legs. Cut one set of legs in half along broken line. Glue whole set of legs lengthways under top. Glue half legs at right angles to them. Paint or varnish table to match chairs.

Sideboard

Cut out front, back, top, top decoration and two sides 4 × 4cm ($1\frac{6}{10}$″ × $1\frac{6}{10}$″). Smooth rough edges. Glue sides to back. Glue front to sides. Glue on the top. Glue top decoration at back edge of top. Paint or varnish.

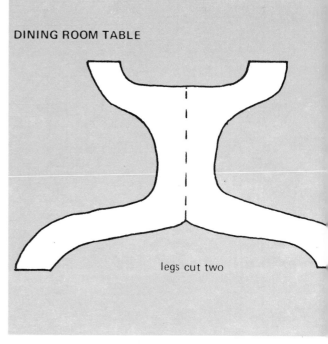

DINING ROOM TABLE

legs cut two

DINING ROOM CHAIR

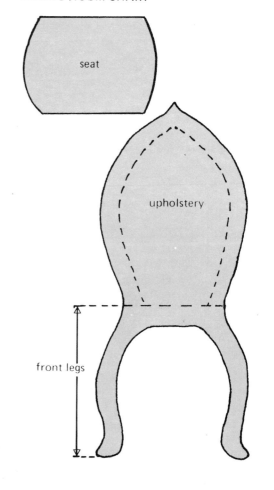

seat

upholstery

front legs

TABLE TOP

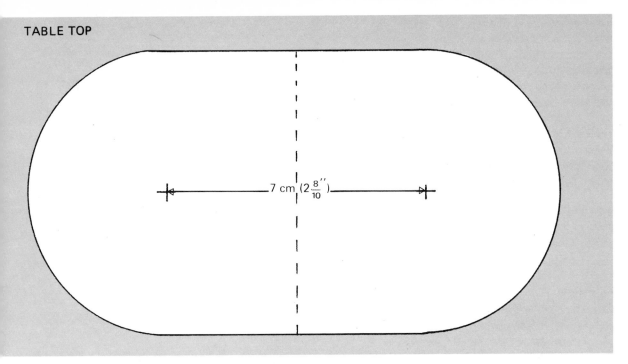

7 cm $(2\frac{8}{10}'')$

SIDEBOARD
front and back

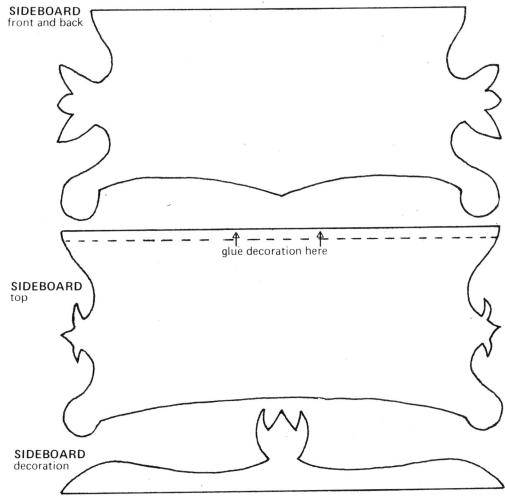

glue decoration here

SIDEBOARD
top

SIDEBOARD
decoration

Drawing room sofa and armchairs

Cut out back, front legs, two arms 1.5 × 3cm ($\frac{6}{10}''$ × $1\frac{1}{10}''$), and seat for each item. Glue seat to back. Glue front legs to seat. Glue arms to back above seat. Upholster back first, then seat, and then arms. The upholstery can be edged with silver or gold cord.

Small table

Cut out top and two sets of legs. Cut one set of legs in half along broken line. Glue legs at right angles to one another. Glue legs to table top.

Stool

Cut out top. Cut out four legs from 6mm ($\frac{1}{4}''$) dowel, and square off. Glue legs to top. Paint or varnish stool, and upholster to match sofa and armchairs.

Aspidistra

Cut ten or twelve leaf shapes from dark green tissue paper. Glue a length of green florist's wire down the back of each leaf. Find a small container to act as a flowerpot. Half fill pot with modelling clay. Push leaf wires into clay at centre. Bend leaves to shape. As these plants were very popular with the Victorians, you could make two or three and place them on a small table in the hall and on the desk in the study.

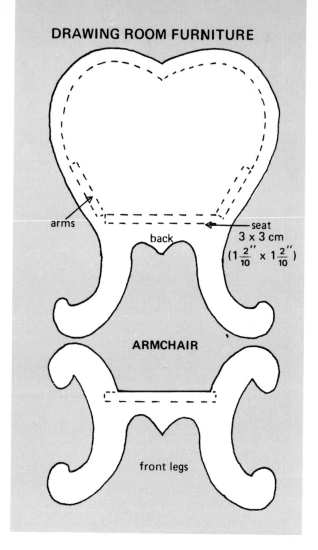

DRAWING ROOM FURNITURE

arms

back

seat
3 x 3 cm
($1\frac{2}{10}''$ x $1\frac{2}{10}''$)

ARMCHAIR

front legs

FOOTSTOOL

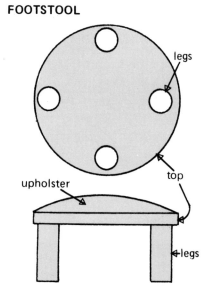

legs

top

upholster

legs

SOFA

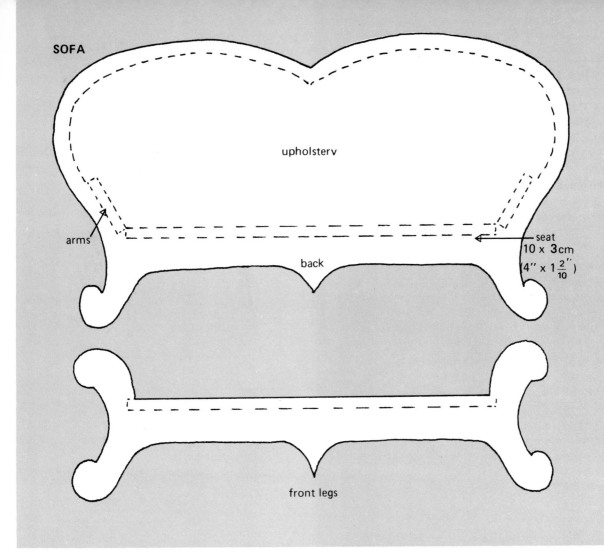

upholsterv

arms

seat
10 × 3cm
(4″ × 1$\frac{2}{10}$″)

back

front legs

SMALL TABLE

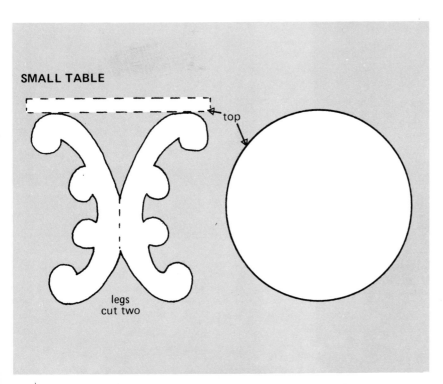

top

legs
cut two

ASPIDISTRA LEAF

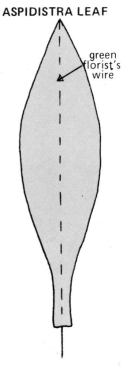

green
florist's
wire

Desk

Cut out four pieces 6 × 4cm ($2\frac{4}{10}'' \times 1\frac{6}{10}''$) for fronts and backs. Cut out four sides 6 × 7cm ($2\frac{4}{10}'' \times 2\frac{6}{10}''$), and top 12 × 7cm ($4\frac{8}{10}'' \times 2\frac{6}{10}''$). Make six drawer fronts and glue to fronts. Glue sides to back. Glue fronts to sides. Glue on the top. Stain and varnish. Glue on beads for drawer handles.

Armchair

Cut out back, seat, and two sides. Glue seat and back to one side. When the glue has set, glue on the other side. Varnish and stain to match desk.

Piano

Cut out back and front, two sides 10 × 3.4cm ($4'' \times 1\frac{4}{10}''$), top 4.5 × 11cm ($1\frac{8}{10}'' \times 4\frac{4}{10}''$), keyboard 8.4 × 2cm ($3\frac{4}{10}'' \times \frac{8}{10}''$), keyboard back 8.4 × 1.5cm ($3\frac{4}{10}'' \times \frac{6}{10}''$) and two front legs. Glue sides to front and back to make open ended box. Glue on the top. Glue front legs in place. Glue keyboard back between legs as shown. Mark out keys on strip of card and glue onto keyboard. Glue keyboard in place. Prime and seal wood, then paint with black gloss paint.

Piano stool

Cut one set of legs and one half set. Cut the first set in half. Glue three legs to top as shown in drawing. Stain and varnish.

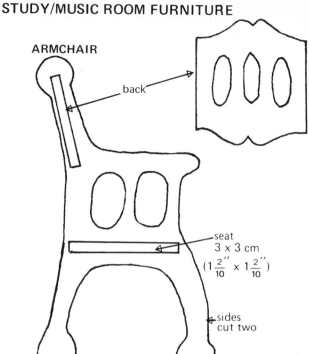

ARMCHAIR

back

seat
3 × 3 cm
($1\frac{2}{10}'' \times 1\frac{2}{10}''$)

sides
cut two

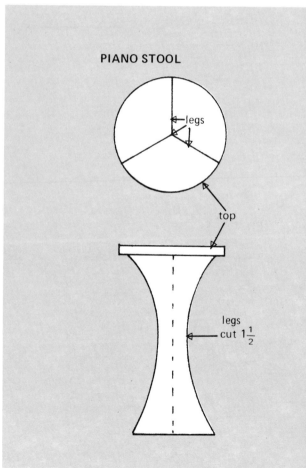

PIANO STOOL

legs

top

legs
cut $1\frac{1}{2}$

DESK

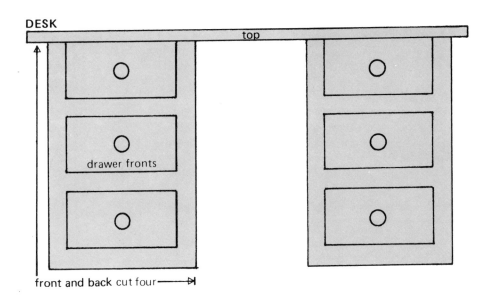

top

drawer fronts

front and back cut four ▸◂

PIANO

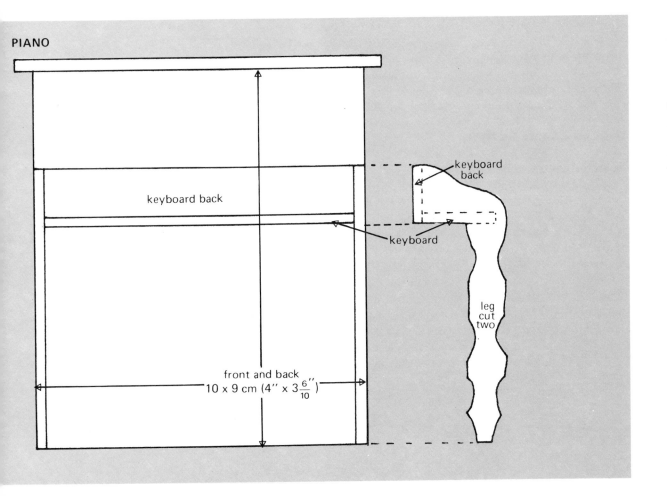

keyboard back

keyboard back

keyboard

front and back
10 x 9 cm (4″ x 3$\frac{6}{10}$″)

leg
cut
two

Kitchen chairs

Cut out back and back legs as one piece. Cut out area between broken lines for front legs, and seat 3 × 3.5cm ($1\frac{2}{10}''$ × $1\frac{4}{10}''$). Glue seat to front legs and then to chair back. Stain and varnish, or paint.

Table

Cut out top 11 × 7.5cm ($4\frac{4}{10}''$ × 3″) and two sets of legs. Glue legs each end of the table about 1cm ($\frac{4}{10}''$) in from edge. Glue strips of wood 8.4 × 1cm ($3\frac{4}{10}''$ × $\frac{4}{10}''$) between legs as shown in plan.

Dresser

Cut out two sides, back 14 × 9.6cm ($5\frac{6}{10}''$ × $3\frac{8}{10}''$), front 6.5 × 9cm ($2\frac{6}{10}''$ × $3\frac{6}{10}''$), cupboard top and bottom 5 × 9cm (2″ × $3\frac{6}{10}''$), three shelves 2.5 × 9cm (1″ × $3\frac{6}{10}''$), and pediment. Glue three shelves to both sides. Glue on back, then add cupboard top and bottom. Glue pediment along top edge of dresser.

Sink and drainer

Make the sink first. Cut out two sides 2.5 × 4.4cm (1″ × $1\frac{4}{10}''$), front and back 2.5 × 7.5cm (1″ × 3″), two legs 3.5 × 5cm ($1\frac{4}{10}''$ × 2″), and bottom 6.9 × 4.4cm ($2\frac{8}{10}''$ × $1\frac{8}{10}''$). Glue the sides to the front and back. Glue bottom in place. Glue legs to sink. Glue strip 4.4cm × 6mm × 6mm ($1\frac{8}{10}''$ × $\frac{1}{4}''$ × $\frac{1}{4}''$) along left side of sink. This supports drainer. Cut drainer leg 5.5 × 5cm ($2\frac{2}{10}''$ × 2″) from 6mm ($\frac{1}{4}''$) ply. Cut drainer top 5 × 7cm (2″ × $2\frac{8}{10}''$). Glue leg to drainer top and lean drainer on sink support. Paint.

Kitchen stove

This plan is shown half size. Cut out four side pieces. In two of these drill three holes about 5mm ($\frac{1}{4}''$) from front edge and 1cm ($\frac{4}{10}''$) apart, so that 5cm (2″) nails can be pushed through the holes. Cut out back and the two front pieces. Glue left side, left front and one side with holes (holes to front) onto back. Push the three nails through the holes in the second drilled side. Feed points of nails through holes in side already glued to back, then glue second side to back. Quickly glue on right front and last side. Line sides up squarely before glue sets. Glue on tops of stove. Cut a shelf to fit between sides and under bars, and glue in place. Paint stove black.

KITCHEN CHAIR

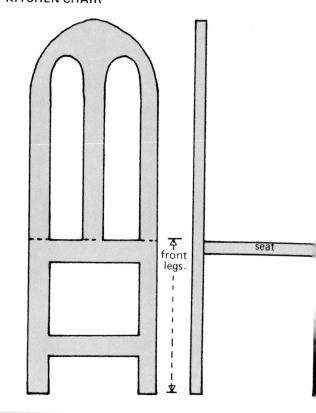

KITCHEN TABLE

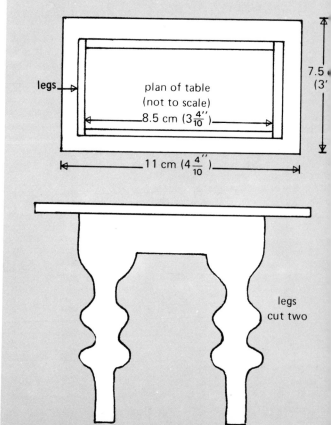

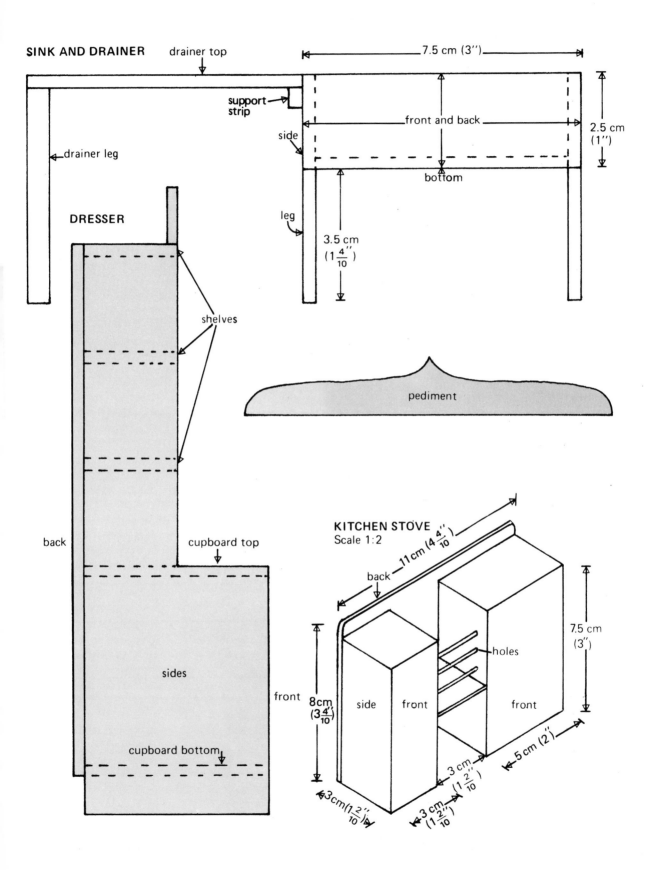

SINK AND DRAINER

drainer top

7.5 cm (3'')

support strip

side

front and back

2.5 cm (1'')

drainer leg

bottom

leg

DRESSER

3.5 cm ($1\frac{4}{10}$'')

shelves

pediment

back

cupboard top

KITCHEN STOVE
Scale 1:2

11 cm ($4\frac{4}{10}$'')

back

holes

7.5 cm (3'')

sides

front

8 cm ($3\frac{4}{10}$'')

side

front

front

5 cm (2'')

cupboard bottom

3 cm ($1\frac{2}{10}$'')

3 cm ($1\frac{2}{10}$'')

3 cm ($1\frac{2}{10}$'')

Bedroom furniture

Each bedroom can have its own washstand, wardrobe, and chest of drawers. The construction of each of these items is described; different suites of furniture can be made by using different finishes.

Washstand

Cut out top 7.5 × 5cm (3″ × 2″), two sides 5 × 4.5cm (2″ × $1\frac{8}{10}$″), back 5 × 7.5cm (2″ × 3″), and lower shelf. Glue lower shelf between sides. Glue sides to top and then to back. Stain and varnish, or paint. For extra decoration, use decals or transfers.

Half-tester bed

This bed is for the main bedroom. Cut out head, foot, and top. Cut out two sides 4 × 15cm ($1\frac{6}{10}$″ × 6″), and mattress base 8 × 15cm ($3\frac{2}{10}$″ × 6″). Glue two sides to head and foot. Then glue mattress base in place. Glue top to edge of head as marked. This gives basic structure of bed, which can now be painted and decorated. Paint with white emulsion paint. Glue fringe around wavy edge of top extension and sides. Glue mattress and two pillows to base. Gold leaves from a cake doily can be mounted on the foot of bed, and gold gift-wrap cord glued around the edges.

Chest of drawers

Cut out top 8 × 5cm ($3\frac{2}{10}$″ × 2″), front and back 6 × 7cm (2″ × 2″), and two sides 4 × 6cm ($1\frac{6}{10}$″ × $2\frac{4}{10}$″). Glue front, back, and sides together. Glue on the top. Cut three drawer fronts to size shown, and glue to front. After staining and varnishing, or painting, glue on beads for drawer handles.

BEDROOM FURNITURE

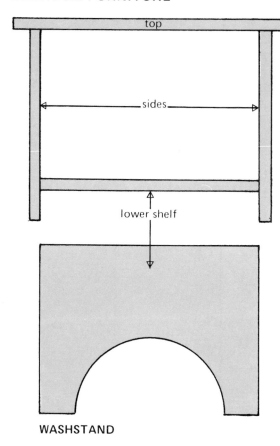

WASHSTAND

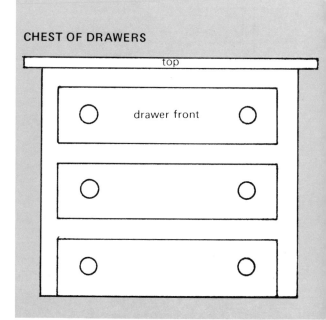

CHEST OF DRAWERS

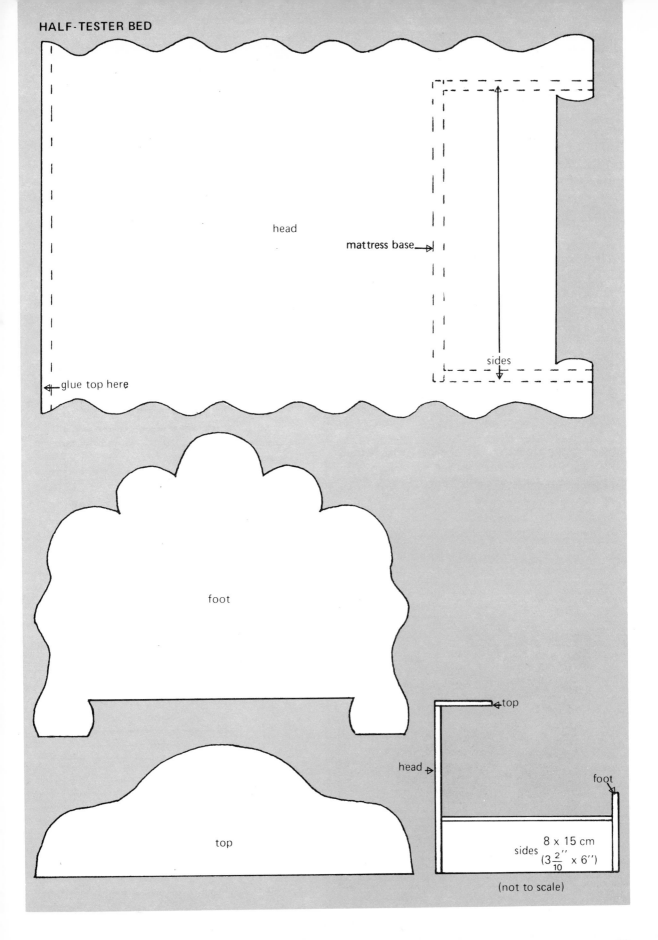

head

mattress base

sides

glue top here

foot

top

top

head

foot

sides

8 x 15 cm
$(3\frac{2}{10}'' \times 6'')$

(not to scale)

Child's bed

Cut out head, foot, and base 5×8cm ($2'' \times 3\frac{2}{10}''$). Glue base between head and foot. Paint. Make a mattress and pillow and glue in place.

Nursery table

Cut out top 9×9cm ($3\frac{6}{10}'' \times 3\frac{6}{10}''$) and four strips 7×1cm ($2\frac{8}{10}'' \times \frac{4}{10}''$). Glue strips under table top to form 7cm ($2\frac{8}{10}''$) square. Cut four legs 4.5×1cm ($1\frac{8}{10}'' \times \frac{4}{10}''$) from 6mm ($\frac{1}{4}''$) plywood. Glue legs inside corners of square formed by strips. Paint or varnish.

Four poster bed

For the base make a box to the dimensions shown on the small drawing. Cut out a mattress base 10×12cm ($4'' \times 4\frac{8}{10}''$) and a top 10×12cm ($4'' \times 4\frac{8}{10}''$). Clamp these two pieces together and drill holes in the corners as shown in the diagram. Glue the mattress base to the box. Cut four lengths of 6mm ($\frac{1}{4}''$) dowel. Glue dowel rods into the top and mattress base. Before the glue is dry check that the dowels are at right angles to the bed and that the top is really horizontal.

After painting, decorate the bed. Glue gauze curtains under the top and tie them to the posts with silver or gold cord. Stick wooden beads on top of the posts, and glue fringe around the edge of the top.

CHILD'S BED

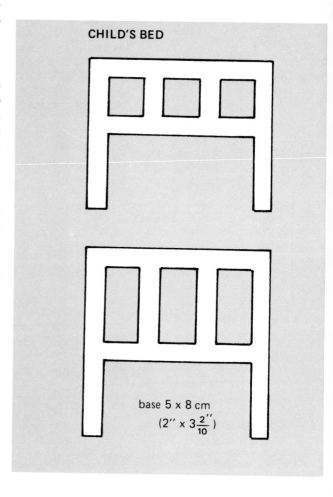

base 5 x 8 cm
($2'' \times 3\frac{2}{10}''$)

NURSERY TABLE

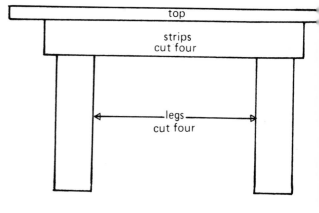

top

strips
cut four

legs
cut four

FOUR POSTER BED

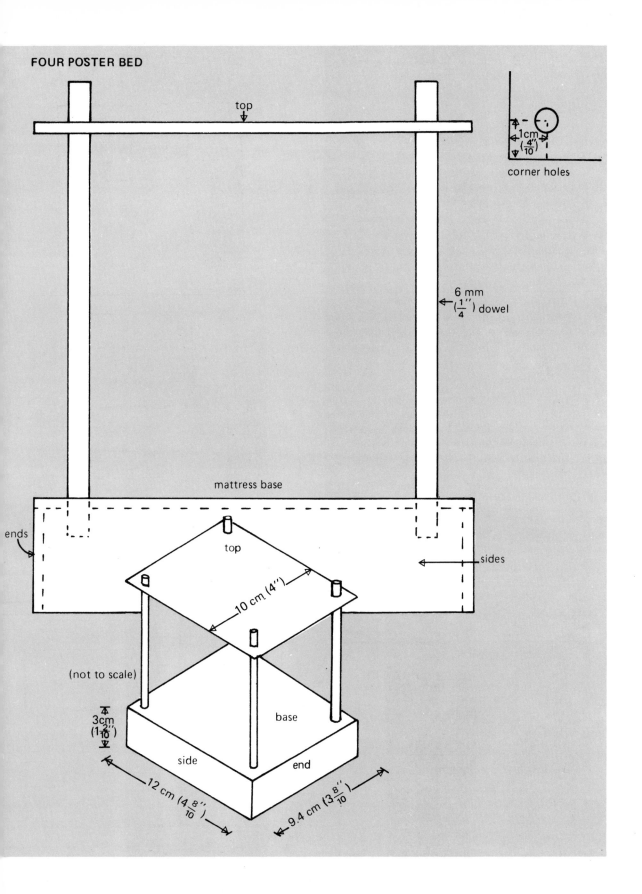

top

corner holes

1cm
($\frac{4''}{10}$)

6 mm
($\frac{1''}{4}$) dowel

mattress base

ends

top

sides

10 cm (4'')

(not to scale)

base

3cm
(1$\frac{2''}{10}$)

side

end

12 cm (4 $\frac{8''}{10}$)

9.4 cm (3$\frac{8''}{10}$)

Cradle

Cut out two ends and two sides. Glue sides and ends together. Cut out the bottom—the size of this is best found after the sides and ends have been glued together. Bend short length of wire to shape shown in drawing, and glue in place with epoxy-resin adhesive. Decorate cradle with lace and thin gauze.

Wardrobe

Cut out back, front and two sides 15×5cm ($6'' \times 2''$), and glue together. Cut two door fronts and glue to doors. Cut top 11×6cm ($4\frac{4}{10}'' \times 2\frac{4}{10}''$) and glue in place. Measure bottom opening and cut wood to size and glue in place. Make plinth from 1cm ($\frac{4}{10}''$) strips, making them 8cm ($3\frac{2}{10}''$) long for front and back and 4cm ($1\frac{6}{10}''$) long for sides. Glue together under wardrobe.

Dressing table

Different dressing tables can be made by using the same basic design and altering the shape of the mirror mount.

Cut out front, back and two sides 6×6cm ($2\frac{4}{10}'' \times 2\frac{4}{10}''$). Glue together. Glue on drawer fronts and beads for handles. Cut top 7×9cm ($2\frac{8}{10}'' \times 3\frac{6}{10}''$) and glue in place. Glue mirror mount level with back of top. Glue mirror of kitchen foil backed with card to mirror opening.

Fireplaces

The photograph below shows two examples of fireplaces. The larger one is as high as the room, 10cm ($4''$) across and 2.5cm ($1''$) deep. The mantelpiece is 10cm ($4''$) from the floor.

The smaller fireplace is $10 \times 10 \times 2.5$cm ($4'' \times 4'' \times 1''$). Decorate the mantelpiece with braid or fringe.

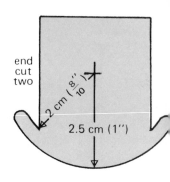

CRADLE

end cut two

2 cm ($\frac{8}{10}''$)

2.5 cm ($1''$)

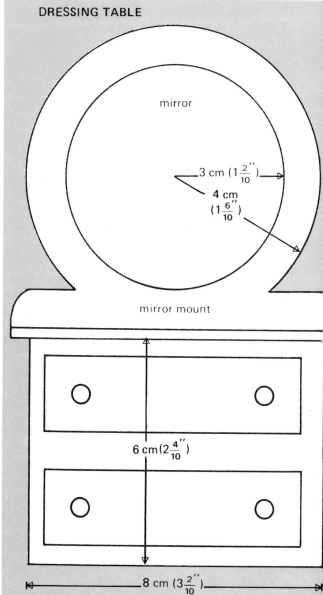

DRESSING TABLE

mirror

3 cm ($1\frac{2}{10}''$)

4 cm ($1\frac{6}{10}''$)

mirror mount

6 cm ($2\frac{4}{10}''$)

8 cm ($3\frac{2}{10}''$)

96

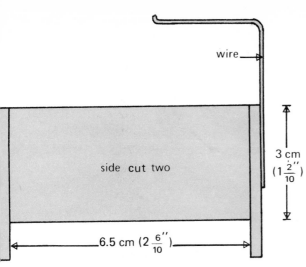

wire

side cut two

3 cm $(1\frac{2}{10}'')$

6.5 cm $(2\frac{6}{10}'')$

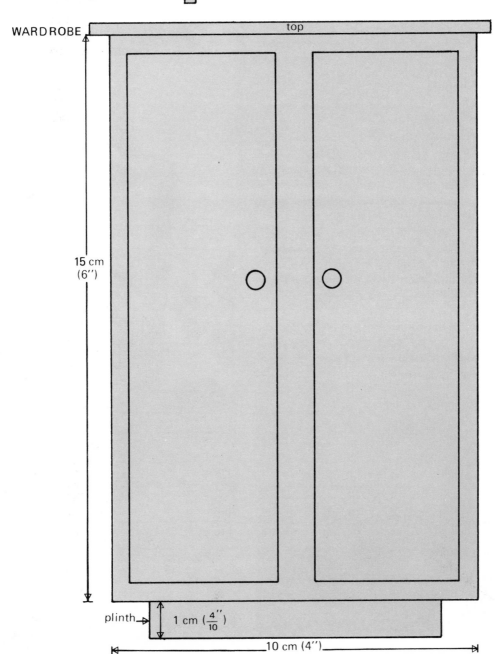

WARDROBE

top

15 cm (6'')

plinth

1 cm $(\frac{4}{10}'')$

10 cm (4'')

THE JAPANESE HOUSE

The inner and outer frames are made of posts and cross spars of square hardwood, and are set into the base.

The design and structure of a Japanese house and garden are deceptively simple. The materials used are those that are easily available, as well as light-weight or able to withstand earthquakes. Most houses are built of untreated timber. Japan has a fairly damp climate, so the houses are raised above the ground. The supports that hold the floor above the ground also support the roof at the top. The roof overlaps the verandah, which surrounds the house and is used for exercise when the weather is poor.

Rooms open onto the verandah by means of sliding screens called *fusuma*, which can be removed to allow freer air circulation in hot, humid weather. The rooms are divided by other sliding screens called *shoji*. Glass is rarely used for glazing, and the screens are covered with translucent paper. Rooms are not usually kept for one specific purpose. The general living area is usually the largest room, but the size of rooms can be changed by moving the screens. The floors of all the rooms are covered with straw mats called *tatami*, and there is very little furniture.

The garden is an extension of the house. It has few flowers. Trees, bushes, rocks, pools or lakes, and islands are carefully placed to provide beautiful views from particular vantage points.

The sliding doors fit into commercially produced tracks that are glued to the base and the inner frame.

The fence is made of plywood and glued between the frame posts.

The simple garden, with lake, island, bridges and trees, provides an extra play area.

Building
the Japanese house

Materials

1 sheet 6mm ($\frac{1}{4}''$) plywood 240 × 120cm (8′ × 4′)
1 sheet 3mm ($\frac{1}{8}''$) plywood 240 × 120cm (8′ × 4′)
5m (18′) 1.5cm ($\frac{5}{8}''$) square hardwood
5m (18′) 1.2cm ($\frac{1}{2}''$) square hardwood
4 sheets thick cardboard 64 × 52cm (26″ × 21″)
2.5m (8′) upper sliding glass door track
2.5m (8′) lower sliding glass door track
1 kilogramme (2 lbs) Plaster of Paris,
cottonwool, green cold water dye, pipecleaners,
florist's wire, green tissue paper, paint
woodworking glue

Posts for outer frame

Cut four 25cm (10″) lengths from 1.5cm ($\frac{5}{8}''$) square
hardwood. Mark line across each post 5cm (2″) from
one end (will be lower end). Mark second line 6mm
($\frac{1}{4}''$) below it. (If your plywood is not exactly 6mm
($\frac{1}{4}''$) you will need to alter last measurement.) Con-
tinue both lines for 7.5mm ($\frac{5}{16}''$) on two adjoining
sides (see diagram). Saw down lines and remove
waste wood, leaving slot halfway through wood
into which plywood base will fit.

Cut six intermediate posts 24.25cm ($9\frac{11}{16}''$) long from
1.5cm ($\frac{5}{8}''$) square hardwood. Cut slots in these to
correspond with those in corner posts.

The base

Cut out rectangle 63 × 48cm ($25\frac{1}{4}'' \times 19\frac{1}{4}''$) from
6mm ($\frac{1}{4}''$) ply. Cut notches 1.5cm × 7.5mm ($\frac{5}{8}'' \times$
$\frac{5}{16}''$) in base at equal distances along sides and in
centre of short sides. All posts should fit square and
flush to base, lifting it 5cm (2″) above ground.

Cut four holes in base 7.5cm (3″) in from each side.
The holes should be 1.2cm ($\frac{1}{2}''$) square, or very
slightly smaller to make tight fit for inner frame.

Cross spars

From 1.5cm ($\frac{5}{8}''$) square hardwood cut two spars
45cm (18″) long for short sides, and two 60cm (24″)
for long sides. Cut notches 1.5cm ($\frac{5}{8}''$) wide and
7.5mm ($\frac{5}{16}''$) deep into which top ends of intermediate posts fit. To find position of notches, align
spars with base and mark positions of posts, but do
not fix in place yet.

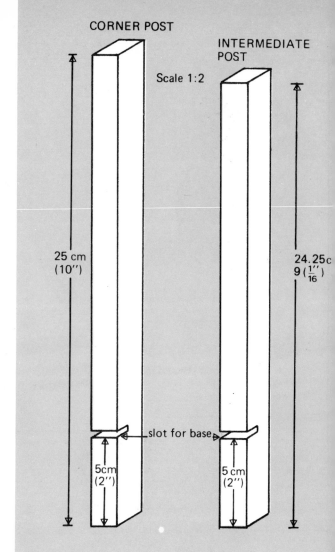

CORNER POST

INTERMEDIATE POST

Scale 1:2

25 cm (10″)

24.25c 9 ($\frac{1}{16}''$)

slot for base

5cm (2″)

5 cm (2″)

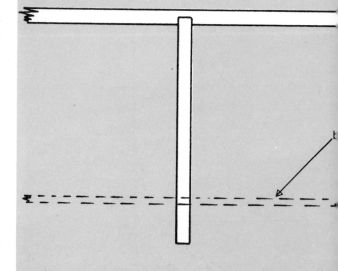

SIDE FRAME

BASE Scale 1:4

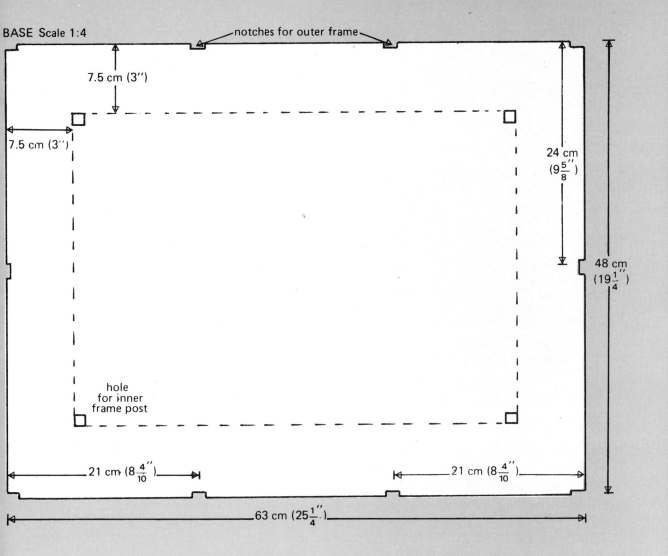

notches for outer frame

7.5 cm (3'')

7.5 cm (3'')

24 cm $(9\frac{5}{8}'')$

48 cm $(19\frac{1}{4}'')$

hole
for inner
frame post

21 cm $(8\frac{4}{10}'')$

21 cm $(8\frac{4}{10}'')$

63 cm $(25\frac{1}{4}'')$

FRONT AND BACK OUTER FRAME

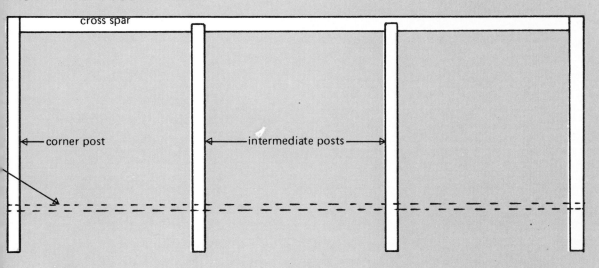

cross spar

corner post

intermediate posts

Check that outer frame fits together squarely. Stain frame with medium dark wood stain. When stain is dry, glue and pin intermediate posts to cross spars. Do not fix corner posts to cross spars or any posts to base yet. Fix outer frame in place after inner frame is in place.

Inner frame

Make inner frame from 1.2cm ($\frac{1}{2}$") square hardwood. Cut 4 corner posts 20.6cm ($8\frac{1}{4}$") long. Posts will stand 20cm (8") above base in line with top of outer frame when fitted in position. Cut slots 6mm ($\frac{1}{4}$") deep and 1.2cm ($\frac{1}{2}$") wide 5cm (2") from top of post.

For front and back inner frames cut two top spars 45.6cm ($18\frac{1}{4}$") long to fit between corner posts. Cut two lower spars 46.8cm ($18\frac{3}{4}$") long and joint them into corner posts 5cm (2") below upper spars.

To make each side frame cut two cross spars 30.6cm ($15\frac{1}{4}$") long. Pin and glue between corner posts as shown in drawing.

Before proceeding further, stain and varnish base. Cover stain with 3 coats of polyurethane varnish. The floor is the only part of house to be varnished.

Fixing frames in place

Stain all parts of inner frame with mahogany stain. When stain is dry, glue and pin front and back inner frames together. Glue in position in base, then pin and glue cross spars of side frames in place. Check that all parts are square to base before glue sets.

Stain outer frame to match floor. Fix in position, checking that all parts are square before glue sets.

Room dividers

Cut two pieces 30.6cm ($15\frac{1}{4}$") long from 1.2cm ($\frac{1}{2}$") square hardwood. Glue one each to upper and lower cross spars of front and back inner frames midway between side frames. Cut two pieces 22cm ($8\frac{8}{10}$") long from 1.2cm ($\frac{1}{2}$") square hardwood. Glue one each to upper and lower cross spars between side frame and middle divider.

Sliding door tracks

Glue upper (deeper) track under lower cross spars of inner frame. Glue lower sliding track to floor directly under upper track. Fit track all round inner frame and under room dividers.

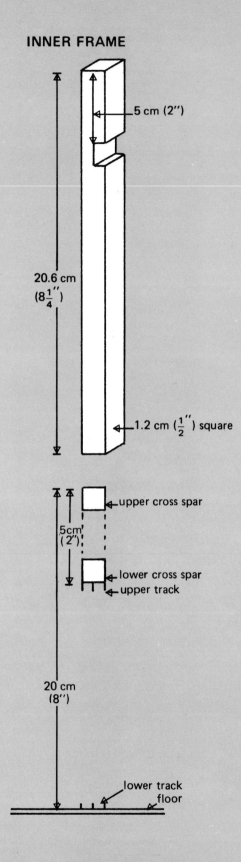

INNER FRAME

5 cm (2")

20.6 cm ($8\frac{1}{4}$")

1.2 cm ($\frac{1}{2}$") square

5cm (2")

upper cross spar

lower cross spar
upper track

20 cm (8")

lower track
floor

FRONT AND BACK FRAMES

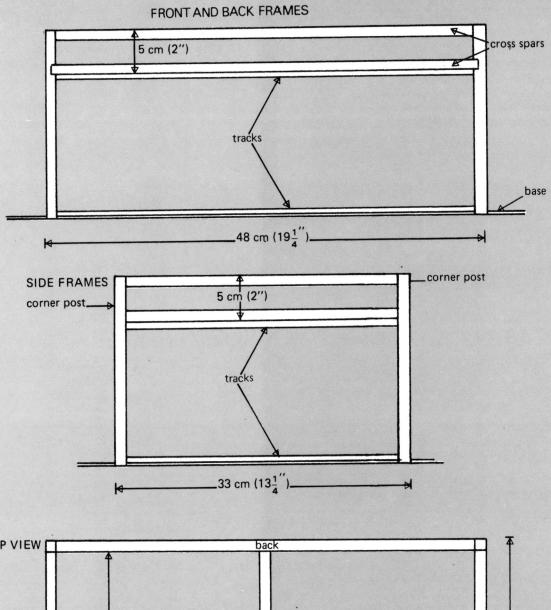

5 cm (2″)

cross spars

tracks

base

48 cm (19$\frac{1}{4}$″)

SIDE FRAMES

corner post

corner post

5 cm (2″)

tracks

33 cm (13$\frac{1}{4}$″)

TOP VIEW

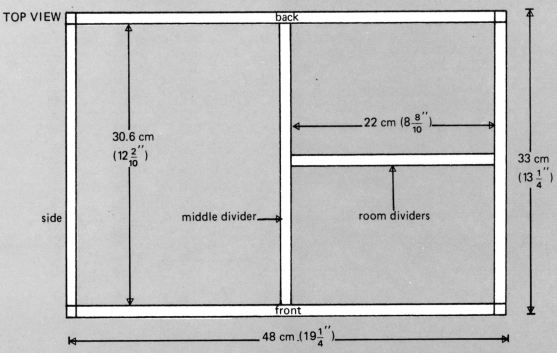

back

22 cm (8$\frac{8}{10}$″)

30.6 cm
(12$\frac{2}{10}$″)

33 cm
(13$\frac{1}{4}$″)

side

middle divider

room dividers

front

48 cm (19$\frac{1}{4}$″)

The roof

Cut roof base 73 × 58cm (29¼″ × 23¼″) from 3mm (⅛″) plywood. This is 5cm (2″) wider all round than floor. To give roof its slightly concave shape, cut roof formers as shown from 6mm (¼″) ply. Copy patterns for roof formers square by square onto 1cm (4/10″) squared paper. Trace onto thin card, cut out and use as templates to draw patterns on plywood.

Cut out central roof former. Cut two slots 6mm (¼″) wide and 11cm (4⅜″) deep as shown.

Cut out two cross formers. Cut slot 6mm (¼″) wide and 11cm (4⅜″) deep as shown.

Cut four corner formers.

ROOF FORMERS Scale 1:4
CENTRAL ROOF FORMER (cut 1)

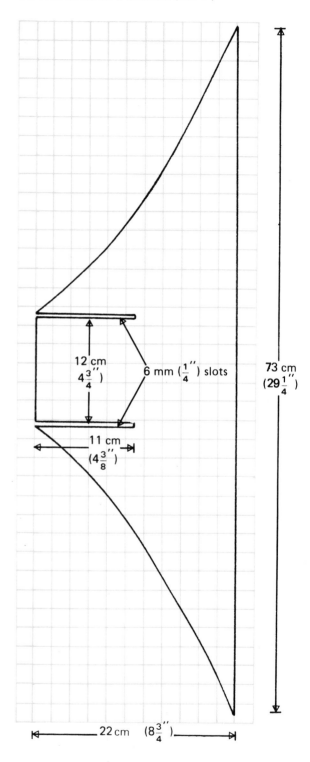

CORNER ROOF FORMER (cut 4: A, B, C, D)

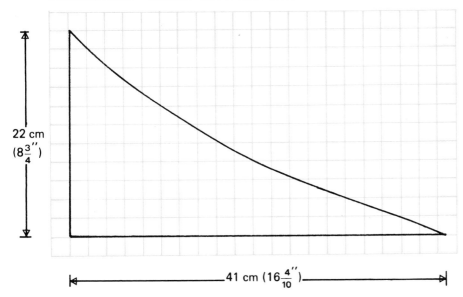

22 cm
($8\frac{3}{4}''$)

41 cm ($16\frac{4}{10}''$)

CROSS FORMER (cut 2)

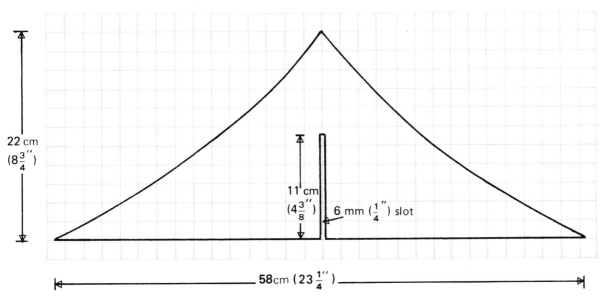

22 cm
($8\frac{3}{4}''$)

11 cm
($4\frac{3}{8}''$) 6 mm ($\frac{1}{4}''$) slot

58 cm ($23\frac{1}{4}''$)

Assembling roof

Pin and glue roof formers to roof base using plan as guide. Cross formers slot into central former. Cover roof with cardboard, one side at a time. The ridges occur along corner formers. Put glue on appropriate formers and push sheet of card onto it. Use drawing pins (thumb tacks) to hold card in place until glue sets. When glue is really dry, trim card to shape with sharp craft knife. Repeat with other sides of roof.

To cover join at top of roof cut strip of card 8×22 cm ($3'' \times 9''$). Fold in half lengthways and glue over top ridge. When dry, trim to shape. To fill in ends, cut oversize card triangles, glue in place, and trim to shape when glue is dry.

Cover side ridges with strips of card 3cm ($1\frac{1}{4}''$) wide, folded in half lengthways. Score fold line before bending. Glue in place and trim corners.

Give roof 2–3 coats of grey emulsion paint. Finish underside of roof with pinewood stain.

Make frame from 1.2cm ($\frac{1}{2}''$) square hardwood to fit loosely round outer frame of house. Glue and pin frame to underside of roof so that when roof is put on house, it is held in place by frame.

Outer sliding doors: shoji

Cut shoji from 3mm ($\frac{1}{8}''$) ply. Check height of door in drawing with your sliding track; cut one door slightly oversize and trim to fit properly in grooves. Push door up into upper grooves as far as it will go; it should now slot into lower groove and still be retained by upper track.

Cut 20 shoji and cover one side of each with tracing or greaseproof paper. Do not stain, paint or varnish.

Inner sliding doors: fusuma

Cut 7 frames from 3mm ($\frac{1}{8}''$) ply. These are same size as shoji, but frame is only 5mm ($\frac{2}{10}''$) all round. Cover both sides of each door with white paper.

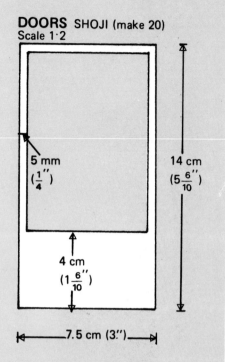

DOORS SHOJI (make 20)
Scale 1·2

5 mm ($\frac{1}{4}''$)

14 cm ($5\frac{6}{10}''$)

4 cm ($1\frac{6}{10}''$)

7.5 cm (3'')

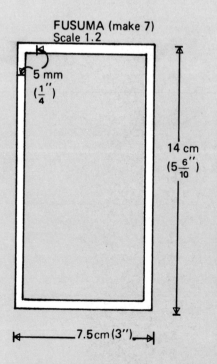

FUSUMA (make 7)
Scale 1.2

5 mm ($\frac{1}{4}''$)

14 cm ($5\frac{6}{10}''$)

7.5cm (3'')

PLAN OF ROOF

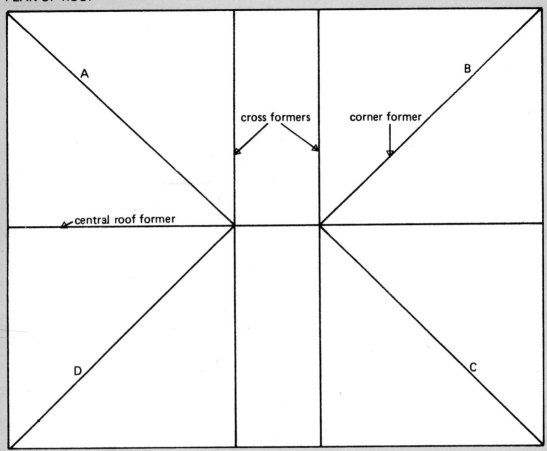

A

B

cross formers

corner former

central roof former

D

C

SIDE RIDGE

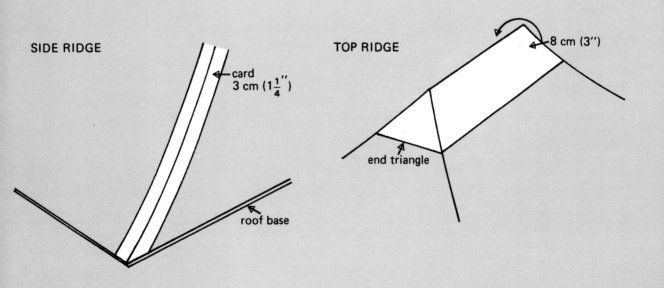

card
3 cm ($1\frac{1}{4}$")

roof base

TOP RIDGE

8 cm (3")

end triangle

Furniture

All furniture is made from 3mm ($\frac{1}{8}''$) plywood and patterns are given full size unless stated otherwise. Trace patterns onto thin card and use these as templates.

There is very little furniture in a Japanese house. There are no chairs, as everyone sits crosslegged on the floor. Tea and food are served on low tables. The beds are sleeping bags that are unrolled and laid on the floor. In every house there is a set of shelves or cupboard in which to store and display artistic treasures such as painted scrolls or a statue of Buddha. Lamp stands support either candles or small oil lamps.

Kimono rack

Cut out main part of rack. Smooth down with fine sandpaper. Cut out two feet and slot them into slots in main part. Glue together and paint black.

Low table

Cut out top and two sets of legs. After smoothing down, glue legs to top a short distance in from ends. Paint black.

Table

Construct higher table in same way as low table. This sort of table is sometimes used as an armrest.

Lamp stands

Cut out base and top, and drill holes through centres to hold dowel rod upright. Cut dowel rod 6cm ($2\frac{1}{4}''$) long. After smoothing rough edges, glue pieces together and paint black.

Shelf unit

Cut strip of 3mm ($\frac{1}{8}''$) ply 3×53cm ($1\frac{2}{10}'' \times 22\frac{1}{4}''$). From this cut 4 sides 8cm ($3\frac{1}{4}''$) long. Glue together to form outer frame. Cut 2 shelves 7.4cm ($3''$) long and 2 shelf supports 3cm ($1\frac{1}{4}''$) long. Glue supports and shelves in place as in drawing, and paint black.

To represent the tatami, or floor mats, cut placemats made from straw or split bamboo to fit rooms.

FURNITURE SHELF UNIT

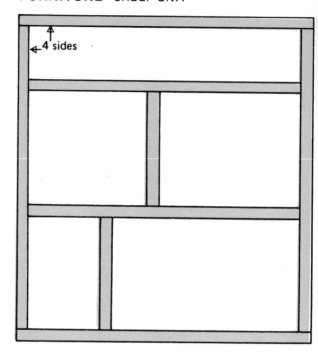

4 sides

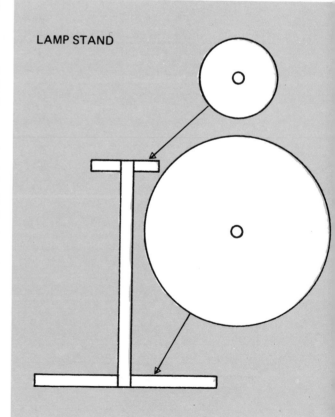

LAMP STAND

KIMONO RACK

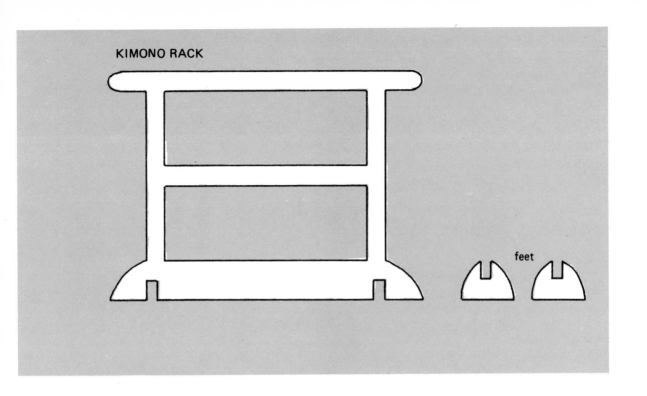

feet

LOW TABLE

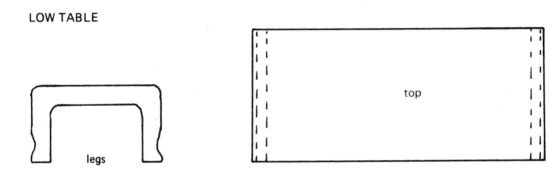

legs

top

TABLE/ARMREST

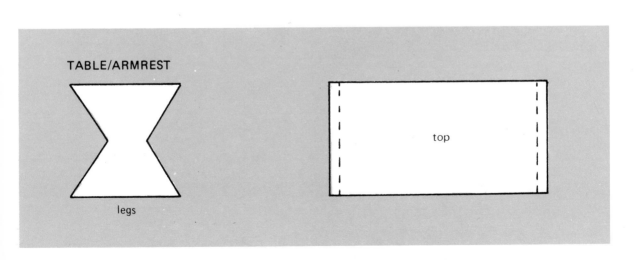

legs

top

Fence

To complete house cut fence from 3mm ($\frac{1}{8}''$) plywood. You will need 8 lengths of pattern shown opposite, but check measurements between posts on your house in case slight alteration is needed. There is no fencing between centre posts front and back. Paint fences with black matt paint and glue in place between posts.

Bridges

Cut two sides from 3mm ($\frac{1}{8}''$) plywood. Cut two arches and glue these to lower inside edge of bridge sides. Cut planks from 6mm ($\frac{1}{4}''$) ply and glue to ridges formed by arches. Make two. Paint white.

FENCE PATTERN

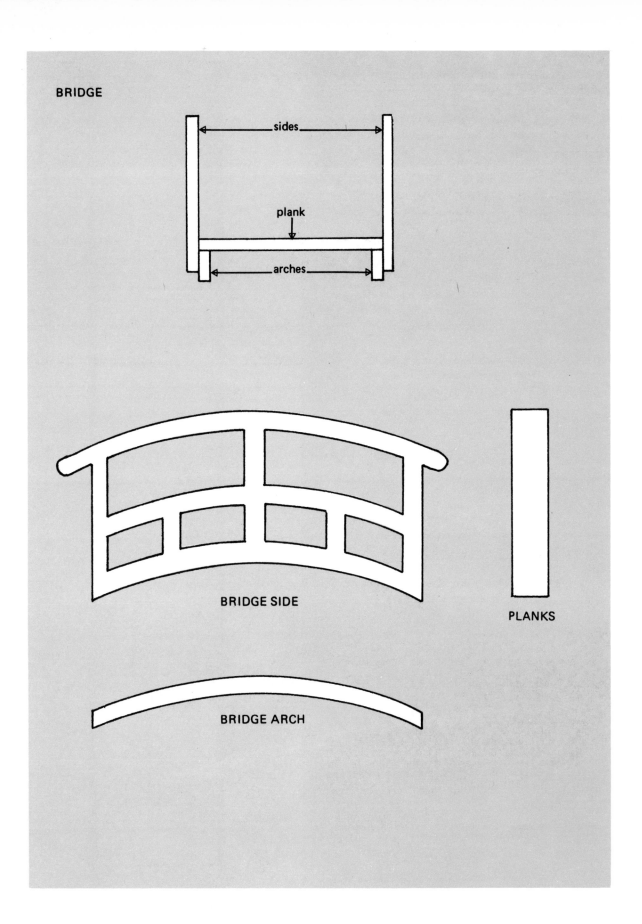

BRIDGE

sides

plank

arches

BRIDGE SIDE

PLANKS

BRIDGE ARCH

The garden

Cut a 75cm (30″) square of 6mm (¼″) plywood. Cut another 75cm (30″) square of 3mm (⅛″) ply.

Mark out shape of lake on 6mm (¼″) ply. Cut out lake using keyhole or pad saw. Cut island from 6mm (¼″) ply. The shapes need not be exactly like those in drawings.

Trace lake pattern onto 3mm (⅛″) ply. Paint this shape with blue-green gloss paint, overlapping edges, to represent water.

On 6mm (¼″) ply build two hills in garden from layers of polystyrene ceiling tile. Cut out bottom layer first, and then next two layers. Glue these together, then glue to base. Cover with Plaster of Paris to make smooth, rounded shape.

Paint cut edges of lake and island brown. Cover garden with grass paper (available in most model-making shops), or paint with grass green emulsion paint.

Glue top layer of garden to bottom layer, matching position of lake and painted area. Paint outer edges of garden brown.

Willow trees

Cut eight lengths of green florist's wire 25–30cm (10″–12″) long. Twist these together tightly for about half their length, and then bend branches to shape. Make base from modelling clay and push tree trunk into it. Leave until clay is dry. Cut leaf shapes from green tissue paper. Stick leaves to branches.

Other trees

Make trunks and branches from pipecleaners. Twist eight pipecleaners together for about two-thirds their length. Bend branches to desired shape. Mount trees on modelling clay bases. When clay is dry, paint brown.

For foliage dye cottonwool with leaf green cold water dye, following manufacturer's instructions. When it is dry, fluff out and glue to branches of trees. If preferred, lichen can be used, as suggested for Hacienda garden.

GARDEN

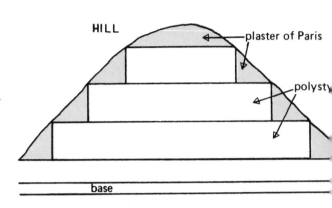

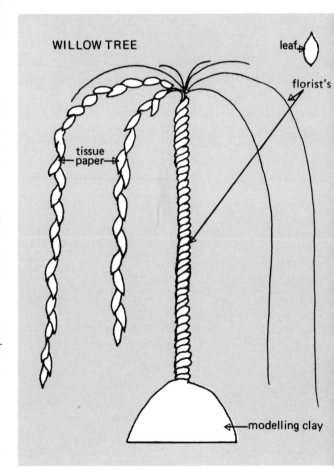

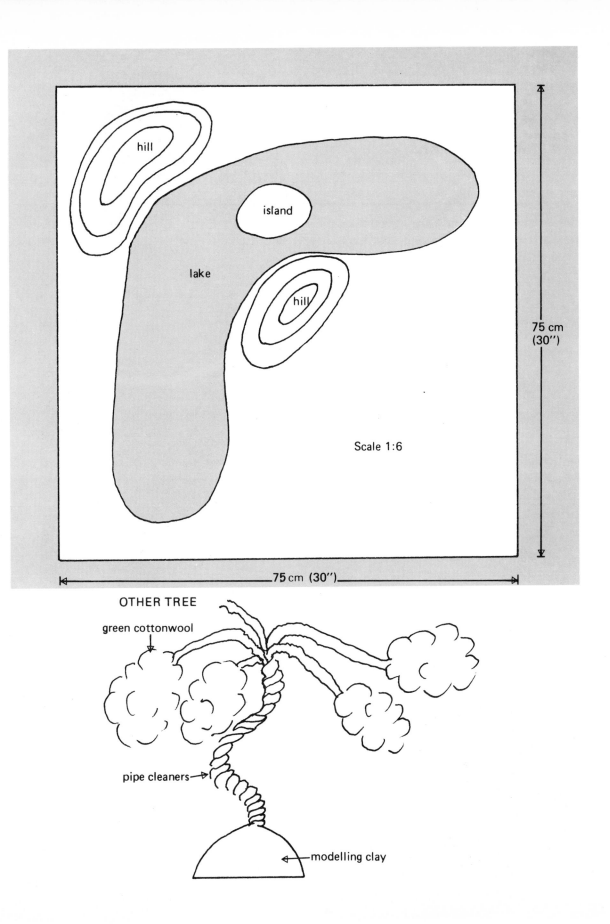

hill

island

lake

hill

75 cm
(30″)

Scale 1:6

75 cm (30″)

OTHER TREE

green cottonwool

pipe cleaners→

modelling clay

THE GYPSY CARAVAN

Gypsies are thought to have originated from somewhere near north-west India about three hundred years ago. No one is sure why they became nomads, but they have reached practically every country in the world.

When the gypsies started their wanderings, they probably used an ox-drawn cart to carry their few belongings. Gradually, the cart developed into the horse-drawn caravan, a house on wheels. Over the centuries gypsies have become masters at the art of building beautiful yet functional homes on wheels. They have learnt how to make the best use of the restricted room inside the caravan.

The inside of the caravan shows the earliest use of fitted furniture. Some of the furniture, such as the cupboards and bench seats, are often integral parts of the caravan structure. The true gypsy shows intense pride in his home; the inside is kept spotlessly clean and the outside is very carefully decorated. Gold, red, and yellow seem to be the favourite colours for painting the outer walls. The outside timbers are often carved and the carvings carefully picked out in various colours.

114

*The curved roof is attached to the caravan wall
with two rebated hinges.*

*The balsa wood window
frames are set into the
upper part of the
caravan walls.*

*The wheels are attached
to an axle, so the
caravan is mobile.*

Building
the caravan

Materials

1 sheet 6mm ($\frac{1}{4}$″) ply 120 × 120cm (4′ × 4′)
1 sheet 3mm ($\frac{1}{8}$″) ply 120 × 120cm (4′ × 4′)
1m (3′) balsa wood 3 × 6mm ($\frac{1}{8}$″ × $\frac{1}{4}$″)
1m (3′) balsa wood 3mm ($\frac{1}{8}$″) square
50cm (18″) of 1.2 ($\frac{1}{2}$″) dowel rod
1.5cm (2″) long 6mm ($\frac{1}{4}$″) coach bolts, 2 washers and
    butterfly nut to fit
1.8cm ($\frac{3}{4}$″) panel pins
2 6mm ($\frac{1}{4}$″) hinges with screws to fit
6 2.5cm (1″) brass hinges with screws to fit
woodworking glue and fabric adhesive
paint, foam rubber, fabric, and trimmings

The basic structure

Cut out base, front, back and two sides from 6mm
($\frac{1}{4}$″) plywood. To make top curve on front and back,
place compass point midway along bottom edge, as
shown, and with a radius of 23.5cm ($9\frac{4}{10}$″) draw arc
from side to side. Draw arc first on a piece of stiff
card, cut out and use as a template for all the curves.

Carefully cut door from front. Using a fretsaw, cut
out upper window opening. Cut door across as
shown to give an upper door with window and a
lower, solid door. Remove all window openings
from sides and back.

Cut a strip 2.5cm (1″) deep from top on front, back,
and two sides. These four strips form roof frame.
Cutting lines are shown by solid lines on drawings.

Glue and pin back to base. Glue and pin two sides
to base and back. Finally, glue and pin front to base
and to ends of sides.

Make outer window frames from 6mm ($\frac{1}{4}$″) balsa
wood and inner frames from 3mm ($\frac{1}{8}$″) square balsa.
Patterns for window frames are shown full size.
Draw them out on paper and build frames over
drawings. Make frames very slightly larger than
window openings and trim to make a really tight
fit when you fix them in place. Note that window
in front door is different from other five windows.
Glue frames together with balsa cement. When glue
is dry, smooth frames with sandpaper, and seal with
coat of emulsion paint. Give frames two coats of
gloss paint and leave to dry. Do not fix in place yet.

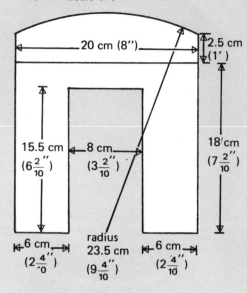

FRONT Scale 1:4

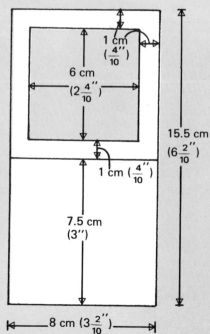

DOOR Scale 1:2

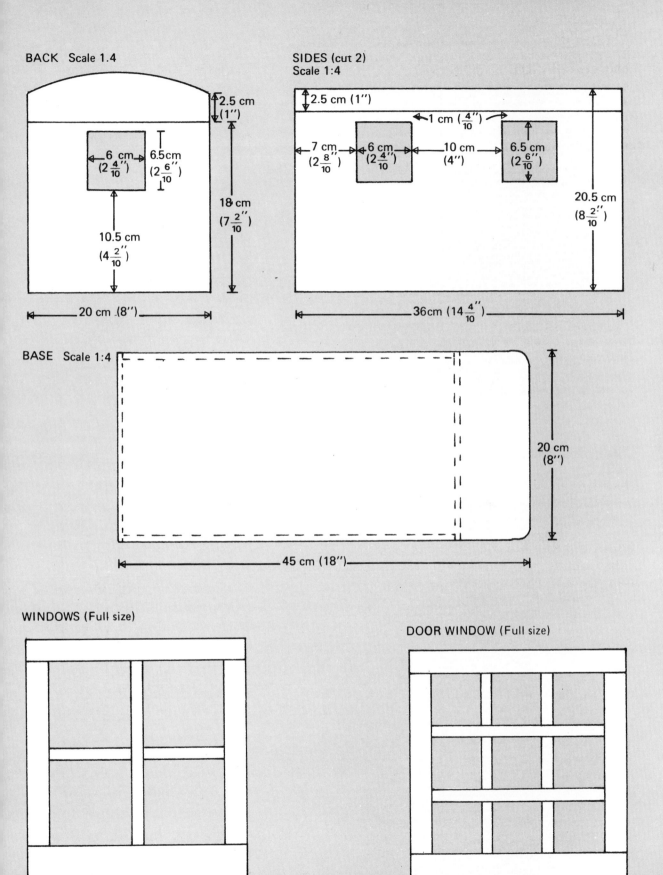

BACK Scale 1:4

2.5 cm (1")

6 cm (2 4/10") 6.5cm (2 6/10")

10.5 cm (4 2/10")

18 cm (7 2/10")

20 cm (8")

SIDES (cut 2)
Scale 1:4

2.5 cm (1")

1 cm (4/10")

7 cm (2 8/10") 6 cm (2 4/10") 10 cm (4") 6.5 cm (2 6/10")

20.5 cm (8 2/10")

36cm (14 4/10")

BASE Scale 1:4

20 cm (8")

45 cm (18")

WINDOWS (Full size)

DOOR WINDOW (Full size)

117

The roof

Cut roof from 3mm ($\frac{1}{8}''$) plywood. Join strips cut from back, front, and sides to form roof frame. Cut two roof supports, using template you have made to draw curves. Fit supports into frame at equal distances from ends. Using a plane, take off outer edges of frame so that curved roof will sit neatly on frame. To help plywood roof to curve, use a sharp craft knife to make deep scores down length of underside. Mark position of frame and supports on roof. Hammer in 1.8cm ($\frac{3}{4}''$) panel pins along centres of these lines. Hold underside of roof in steam from boiling kettle. When wood feels supple, put glue on frame, slightly curve roof and fix into place. A second pair of hands is very helpful in carrying out this operation.

When roof is dry, hinge it to one side of caravan. Make sure that roof matches up with all four sides, then mark in position of hinges. Remove thin layer of wood from caravan side and roof frame so that when hinges are fitted, closed roof will rest squarely on caravan walls. Use 2.5cm (1") brass hinges and 1.2cm ($\frac{1}{2}''$) screws. Add epoxy-resin adhesive to give hinges an even better grip.

Front door

Hinge front door and window door in position, using 2.5cm (1") hinges. Rebate hinges as for roof. Remove doors, decorate and fix window frame in position. Rehinge when all outer decoration has been completed.

Outer decoration

Make overlay that decorates outer walls of caravan from 6mm ($\frac{1}{4}''$) square balsa wood. Stick vertical pieces in place first. Complete patterns by sticking horizontal pieces in place.

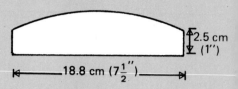

ROOF SUPPORT (Scale 1:4)

2.5 cm (1")

18.8 cm ($7\frac{1}{2}''$)

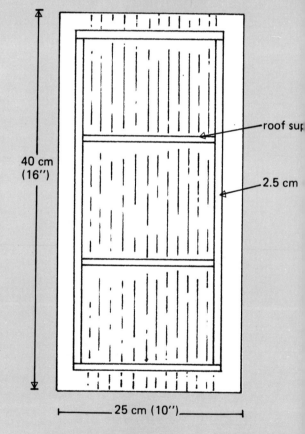

ROOF AND ROOF FRAME

40 cm (16")

roof sup

2.5 cm

25 cm (10")

OVERLAY PATTERNS
FRONT Scale 1:4

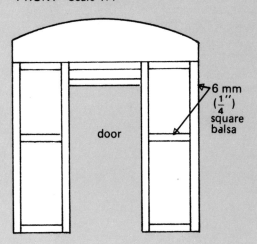

door

6 mm $(\frac{1}{4}'')$ square balsa

REAR Scale 1:4

window

BACK Scale 1:4

window

window

6 mm $(\frac{1}{4}'')$ square balsa

Wheels

Make four wheels and four axle mounts from 3mm ($\frac{1}{8}''$) plywood. Make mounting block 16×10cm ($6\frac{1}{4}'' \times 4''$) from 6mm ($\frac{1}{4}''$) plywood.

Mounting back wheels

Pin straight edge of axle mounts to 10cm (4") edge of mounting block, keeping top edges flush. Make an axle 20cm (8") long from 1.2cm ($\frac{1}{2}''$) dowel rod. Push axle through holes in axle mounts and glue wheels in place. Glue and pin block to underside of caravan about 2.5cm (1") from back and 2cm ($\frac{8}{10}''$) from each side.

Mounting front wheels

Copy shafts pattern square by square onto 1cm ($\frac{4}{10}''$) squared paper. Cut out shafts and 12×10cm ($5'' \times 4''$) mounting block from 6mm ($\frac{1}{4}''$) plywood. Hinge straight edge of shafts to 12cm (5") edge of mounting block with two 6mm ($\frac{1}{4}''$) hinges. Drill hole in middle of block to fit a 6mm ($\frac{1}{4}''$) bolt. Drill similar hole in caravan floor 10cm (4") from front and equidistant from sides. Widen this hole slightly so that bolt head will be recessed. Pass bolt through floor, add washer, pass through mounting block, add washer and screw on wing nut. Make an axle 16cm ($6\frac{1}{4}''$) long from 1.2cm ($\frac{1}{2}''$) dowel rod. Push axle through axle mounts and glue wheels in place.

SHAFTS (Scale 1:2)

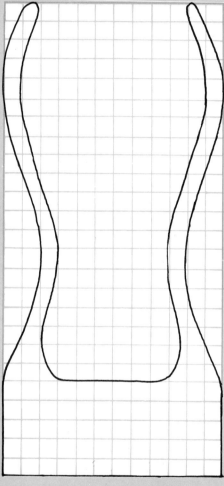

each square represents 1 cm ($\frac{4''}{10}$)

WHEEL (Full size)

AXLE MOUNT (Scale 1:2)

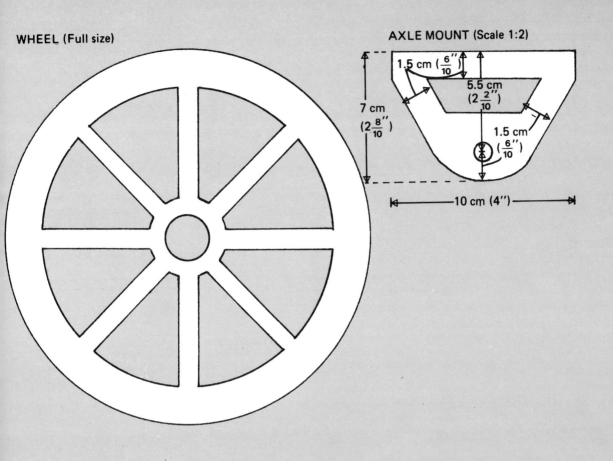

7 cm ($2\frac{8}{10}''$)

1.5 cm ($\frac{6}{10}''$)

5.5 cm ($2\frac{2}{10}''$)

1.5 cm ($\frac{6}{10}''$)

10 cm (4'')

MOUNTING WHEELS AND AXLES (not to scale)

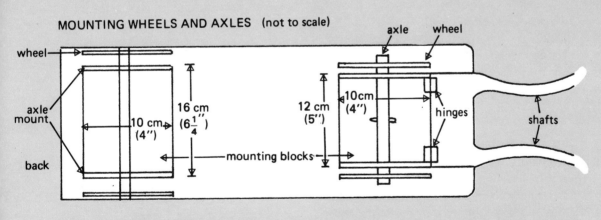

wheel

axle

wheel

axle mount

16 cm ($6\frac{1}{4}''$)

10 cm (4'')

12 cm (5'')

10cm (4'')

hinges

shafts

back

mounting blocks

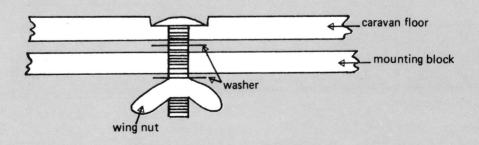

caravan floor

mounting block

washer

wing nut

Decorating

Remove sharp edges with sandpaper and fill holes and cracks with cellulose woodfiller. Seal wood with coat of emulsion paint. When this is dry, apply two or three coats of gloss paint. To decorate panels as in photograph, cut flowers from gift-wrapping paper, glue to panels and cover with coat of polyurethane varnish. Trim overlay and wheels with gold paint.

When the decoration is complete, glue window frames in place and rehinge two parts of front door. Paint floor of caravan or cover with self-adhesive vinyl. Paint walls.

Curtains

Make curtains from pieces of fabric 3×8cm ($1\frac{2}{10}$″ $\times$ $3\frac{2}{10}$″). Gather fabric in middle, using fabric adhesive to hold gathers. Glue curtains to card pelmet (valance) covered with same fabric. Glue pelmet (valance) above window. Make two curtains for each window.

Furniture

Furniture is made from 3mm ($\frac{1}{8}$″) plywood unless stated otherwise. Patterns are given full size; trace them onto thin card and use these as templates. Paint, varnish or stain all furniture.

Bench

Cut out four sides, two backs and two seats 12×3.5cm ($4\frac{8}{10}$″ $\times 1\frac{4}{10}$″). Smooth with sandpaper. Glue seat to sides, and then add back. Hold together firmly until glue has set. Paint with gloss or emulsion paint.

To upholster seats and backs cut pieces of thin card to size. Use these as templates to cut pieces of foam rubber 1cm ($\frac{4}{10}$″) thick. Cut pieces of fabric 1.5cm ($\frac{1}{2}$″) wider all round than templates. Place fabric face down on work surface and put foam rubber and then card in middle of it. Put fabric adhesive on card and pull fabric onto it, being careful to make corners neat. When glue is dry, glue cushions to backs and seats.

Bed

Cut out head, foot, base 10×14cm (4″ $\times 5\frac{6}{10}$″), and two sides 4×14cm ($1\frac{6}{10}$″ $\times 5\frac{6}{10}$″). Join head and foot to sides, and then glue to base. Paint bed. Make and glue on mattresses and pillow in same way as upholstery described above.

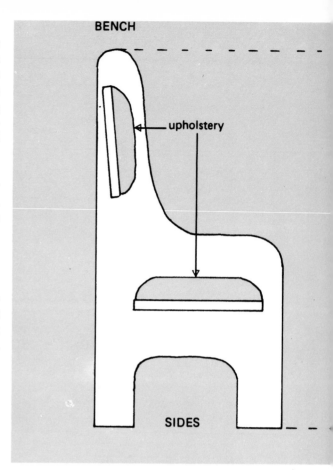

BENCH

upholstery

SIDES

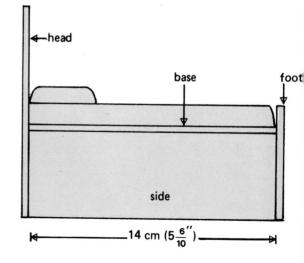

BED
SIDE VIEW (not to scale)

head

base

foot

side

14 cm ($5\frac{6}{10}$″)

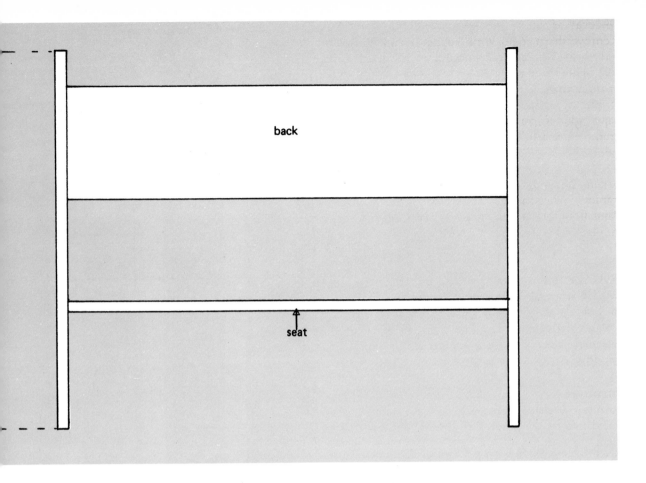

back

seat

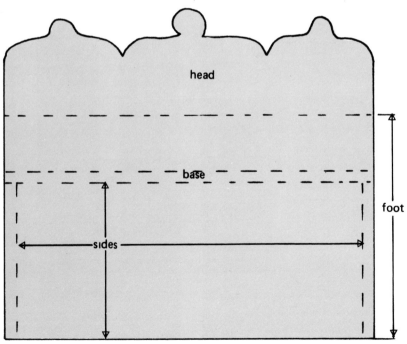

head

base

sides

foot

Dresser

Cut out two sides, top, two top shelves, two bottom shelves, and back 17×9.6cm ($6\frac{8}{10}'' \times 3\frac{8}{10}''$). Glue top and shelves to sides. Glue back in place. Paint.

Table

Cut out top, four legs and four 1cm ($\frac{4}{10}''$) strips to make frame. Glue strips together to make frame. Glue frame under table top and glue legs in place in corners. Paint, or stain and varnish.

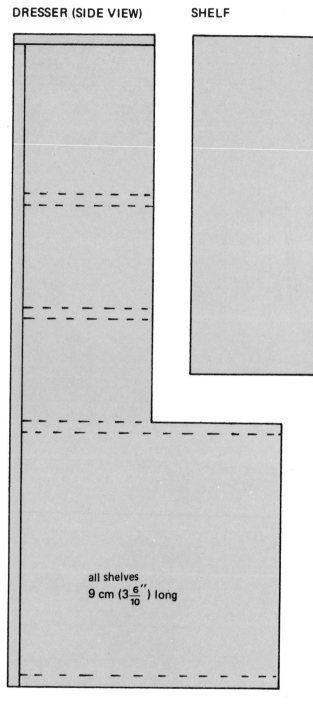

DRESSER (SIDE VIEW)   **SHELF**

all shelves
9 cm ($3\frac{6}{10}''$) long

TABLE

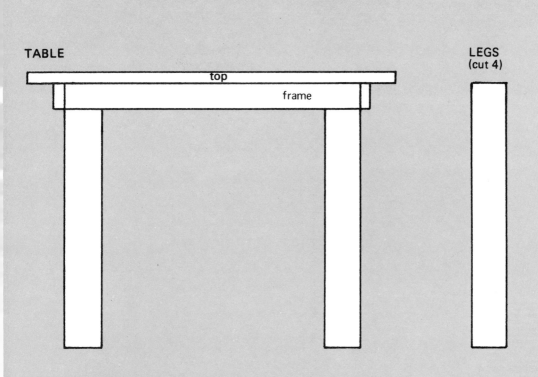

top

frame

LEGS
(cut 4)

VIEW FROM BELOW

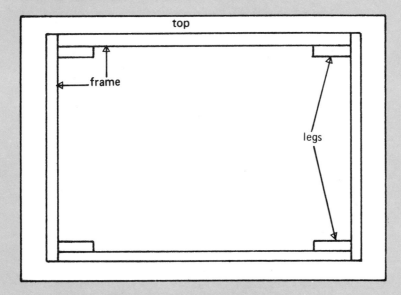

top

frame

legs